A Deed of the Foulest Kind

ENDORSEMENTS

"When Catherine Clark died in 1857, rumors flew in the small town of Danville. Had she been murdered, and by whom? Terry Diener's historical account of the facts of the case make a compelling mystery that will leave you guessing." ~ *Kathleen McQuiston Library Director of the Thomas Beaver Free Library of Danville*

"Terry Diener has created an historical who done it that creates both speculation and suspicion in the mind of the reader! The Foulest of Deeds weaves a page turning tale of murder and mystery amid the backdrop of nineteenth century central Pennsylvania." ~ *Trevor S. Finn, Commissioner, Montour County Board of Commissioners*

A Deed of the Foulest Kind

The 1858 Danville Pennsylvania Murder Cases of William J. Clark and Mary Twiggs

Terry M. Diener

DEDICATION

This book is dedicated to the thousands of iron ore miners, mill workers, and their families, who scraped out a difficult way of life in Montour County. The immigrants from Wales, Ireland, Scotland, Germany, and other countries placed Danville on the map because of their work ethic, perseverance, and desire for a better life. They fulfilled the 1800 prophecy of Danville's Founder General William Montgomery. He said, "These hills are full of iron. There will someday be great iron factories here employing many and yielding boundless wealth."

Contents

x

FORWARD

Terry Diener was first introduced to everyone in Danville, Pennsylvania as a radio announcer for WPGM. Several years later, I met him on a more regular basis when the Iron Heritage Festival (IHF) committee was working to publicize IHF events on the radio. Terry asked wonderfully interesting questions and was instrumental in helping to make our festival one people wanted to attend.

Terry has been a friend for the past twenty years even though I asked him to stand in 100-degree heat and tell the story of James Scarlett, Charles Wetzel, and other historic persons, as a member of the IHF Cemetery Tours. Like a true Thespian, Terry embodied the history of the person he was portraying, and visitors loved listening to his "story."

One of Terry's proudest IHF moments was when he portrayed Colonel Charles Eckman during the summer of 2013. He was invited to escort James Getty, the acclaimed re-enactor who was widely known for his portrayal of Abraham Lincoln, to an Iron Heritage Festival event. The photograph on this page documents that special event.

While Terry has always been interested in local, national, and world history, his work with the Montour County Historic Committee and his work as the author and presenter of podcasts about local history have propelled him to the level of *historian*.

Terry's goal in writing this account is to accurately recall the trials of Mary Twiggs and William Clark, local legends who may – or may not – have been wrongfully convicted of adultery and murder. It is a story you will find to be interesting, compelling, and thought-provoking.

This fascinating account is meticulously researched and Terry relates it in a style that makes it a bit easier to read and understand the events that took place more than 160 years ago.

Jean L. Knouse
March 2020

PREFACE

The reason I wrote this book is to share the true story of two Irish Protestant families who came to America, and eventually to Danville, seeking new lives amid the toil and grime of the rolling mills. Instead, those lives were shattered by scandal, poisonings, and the only two hangings ever carried out in Montour County.

I believe it is fair to say that the events, as they unfolded from the spring of 1857 through the fall of 1858, were *the* talk of the community. Witnesses testified during the trials of William J. Clark and Mary Twiggs, that there was "great talk and flying reports." This story must have been the conversation in front room parlors, on the tongues of street gossipers, and on the lips of workers who toiled in the iron mills of the town, as well as Irish, Welsh, German, Polish and others workers as they drank at their favorite watering holes.

Because 160 years have passed, I relied on immigration records, newspaper accounts, limited court room resources, and information from the Pennsylvania State Archives, to help piece the story together. It is certainly a story worth telling, including the conversations between Mary Twiggs and one of her spiritual advisors in the weeks leading up to her death. Also contained in the book, are letters and petitions from those who would seem to be unlikely supporters, asking Governor William F. Packer to pardon Mrs. Twiggs.

I hope you enjoy the book. I enjoyed gathering the information and will let you form your own opinion on the innocence or guilt of William J. Clark and Mary Twiggs.

~ Terry Diener

CHAPTER 1

It was early September 1858 and the construction of the gallows had been completed to carry out the punishment for those who were convicted of murdering Catherine Ann Clark. At the planing mill where the gallows was built, spectators watched as a bag filled with mud was used to test its efficiency. A local newspaper described the gallows as a "perfect and terrible" instrument and this one was to be used to hang two convicted murderers: a man and a woman.

The final hours in the life of Mary Twiggs the woman for whom the gallows was intended, were heart wrenching. Her children, a boy of about seven and a girl of ten had been allowed to spend the night before her execution with their mother.

And, as only a loving mother could do, she held them in her arms, stroked their hair, spoke lovingly to them and, at times, she sobbed as the minutes of her life slipped away on October 22, 1858. Her daughter appeared to be the most affected, yet, when her mother sometimes cried uncontrollably, the little girl braced herself up and begged, in tender words, that her mother must not cry so much.

Also spending the night with her in the Montour County prison were three women: Mrs. Ware, Mrs. Unger and Mrs. Ephlin. All had come forward to minister to the physical and spiritual needs of the condemned woman and, so, they were witnesses to her final hours.

In the evening before she was to be hanged, Mary rose from her bed and voluntarily knelt down to engage in silent prayer, with apparent fervor and true sincerity – calling audibly at times upon Jesus to save her immortal soul. And when Mrs. Ware engaged in loud prayer, Mrs. Twiggs joined with earnestness in her petitions to the throne of God.

During the night, Mrs. Ephlin questioned the prisoner, at one time pointedly, as to her innocence or guilt of the crime for which she was convicted. Mary Twiggs answered sternly and sharply that she was innocent, quoting at the same time the words of the gospel, "Judge not, lest ye be judged."

Between 11 and 12 o'clock, Mary Twiggs closed her eyes, appearing to sleep, with no sign of restlessness, before arising for her final day at 3 am. When her children awoke, their mother, as she had no doubt done hundreds of times before, carefully dressed them. But this would be the final time Mary Twiggs would be able to "fuss" over her little boy and girl. This would be the last time she would offer motherly attention. She held them close, brushed their hair, and wiped the tears from their faces as well as her own. Those warm hugs and tender embraces would never be felt by her children again.

What were the thoughts racing through the condemned woman's mind? Did the children understand that this was the last time they would feel their mother's touch and look into her loving face before they said goodbye?

After the children's departure, the attention returned to the prisoner when the Sheriff's wife, Mrs. Young, entered the cell with a new black dress in which Mary Twiggs would be hung and buried. The prisoner appeared composed and patiently allowed the ladies to attend to her personal needs.

At about 9 am, Mary's only brother, Samuel McClintock, visited her for the last time. She was seated on the bed of her prison cell when he entered and, as they fell into each other's arms, each cried and sobbed uncontrollably. At first, nothing was spoken, but then the words of "dear, dear sister"— "dear, dear brother"— were heard.

Mrs. Twiggs then focused on Samuel and spoke in broken sentences.

> I know dear brother it is hard to part. My love shall remain with you in the other world. It is hard to part. We have been raised together and always loved each other. My Savior died for us. Don't fret about me, dear brother. I am happy. I'm going to suffer death for others. So did my Savior. Go and love Jesus. Don't believe that I have ever done such a thing. I am innocent, God knows it. He is the judge of all things and knows all things. There will be no injustice in heaven. It will be all love and joy. We all must die. I might have died some other way and then you would have lost me. Now I am prepared. Don't mourn, don't fret dear brother. I hope God will watch over you and

defend you. Don't grieve, I am well, well prepared for heaven.

After unburdening her heart, Mary and her brother shared more calmly in private matters regarding the children. Samuel promised to take care of them. When he cried out again, she tried to comfort him again by saying, "Dear brother you must not grieve so much. We do not see as Jesus sees. If He was only here now to tell, He would tell you that I am innocent. Don't grieve so much about me." During all this time they were seated on her bed, locked tightly in one another's arms, resting their heads upon each other's shoulders.

Before she was led from the cell, the Reverend. A.F. Shanafelt, a Baptist minister from White Hall, Montour County, came forward to offer final spiritual support. After he shared the 51st Psalm, the Reverend M. J. Stover, who had been her principal spiritual advisor during her imprisonment, led a prayer in which all participated.

Reverend Stover than had a few private moments with Mrs. Twiggs, after which a hymn of her selection, "Oh That I Had Some Humble Place Where I Might Hide from Sorrow," was sung. Another of her final requests, the 23rd Psalm, was also read.

Other pastors from the community who had offered support during the woman's lengthy incarceration, attended to her spiritual needs in the final moments in her life. They included a fervent prayer from Reverend Bacon, a Methodist minister. The Reverend Harden led in singing the hymn, "There is a Fountain Filled with Blood, Drawn from Emmanuel's Veins." During this time, Mrs. Twiggs and her brother were still sitting on the bed, weeping audibly, and clinging to one another.

Harden then approached Mary and asked in an affectionate, but earnest, manner whether she was guilty or innocent of the murder of Catherine Clark and warned her of the consequences of deceit and lying in these her last moments on earth. At that time, she disengaged herself from her brother's arms, and firmly said: "I did not tell an untruth during the whole time, and I never contradicted anything I have said. I am ready to abide by the law, and I believe my sins are all forgiven."

Another pastor who was present, the Reverend Mr. Crampton advised her that if she spoke the truth now, she would be rewarded for it hereafter. He followed with a short prayer and commended her soul to God.

Sheriff Young then asked the brother of Mrs. Twiggs to leave the room to allow the sheriff to complete his last duties. As his sobbing continued, Samuel McClintock pleaded, "Save my sister!" He clung to her, but finally had to be forcefully removed from her cell.

Twenty-seven-year-old Mary Twiggs then began her walk to the gallows to fulfill the jury's decree that she be hanged for the murder of Catherine Ann Clark. Her path followed the same one William Clark had walked one month previously when he was sentenced to the gallows for the murder of his wife, Catherine.

The Clarks and Twiggs were neighbors and friends and both Mary Twiggs and William Clark insisted to their dying breath that they were innocent of adultery and murder.

CHAPTER 2

The Irish Potato Famine devastated Ireland between 1845 and 1849. A population of 8.4 million at the start of the famine was reduced to 6.6 million by 1851. However, death by starvation was not the only reason for the decrease in population.

Immigration during those years was a significant factor in the population decline. Pennsylvania became a popular landing spot for immigrating families. Its founder, William Penn, was born to an English nobleman whose family had land holdings in Ireland and he had lived there for several years. Because Penn had seen the harsh treatment of Irish families, and because of his conversion to the Quaker faith, he welcomed immigrant families from many countries to the land he had been granted in America.

William John Clark was born in the town of Morass, Donegal County, Northern Ireland in August of 1834. Clark was 16 years old, and alone, when he boarded a ship in Glasgow, Scotland and sailed to the United States. He arrived in New York City aboard the ***Clydesdale*** on May 11, 1851. On the passenger list, his occupation was listed as "farmer."

William Clark's parents had come to the United States two years before he did. On his arrival, the young Clark worked in a brickyard in New York City before moving to Philadelphia in the fall of 1851. He drove a coal cart and married his wife Catherine Ann on August 27, 1851. In March of 1852, Clark and his family, including their young son, moved to Kittanning in Armstrong County where he worked in a rolling mill operated by Phillips, Brown and Company.

After spending just over two years in western Pennsylvania, Clark moved his family back to Philadelphia, again for two years, and during at least part of that time was working at the Kensington Iron Works.

In November of 1855, Clark, who was probably a skilled iron worker by this time, his wife Catherine and two children, a newborn and a boy of five, arrived in Danville. He was hired as a puddler at the Montour Iron Works. The puddler was responsible for adding various elements to the molten iron at the proper moment and rolling it in order to work out impurities to produce a quality product. He was an important member of the team.

At this time, William Clark still had family living in Philadelphia and his father lived in Sugarcreek Township, Armstrong County.

Clark was raised in the Presbyterian Church and according to later newspaper accounts, was a prominent member of that denomination in Danville. The same news article described him as five feet five inches with a luxuriant crop of black hair and heavy black eyebrows. He had a very low forehead, a small mouth, black eyes, and a pale but fair complexion. Clark was said to have had a downcast look but was also rather intelligent.

Mary McClintock was born to Irish Protestant parents in 1830 in Northern Ireland. A marriage record shows that David Twiggs and Mary McClintock were married in the town of Convoy, in the county of Donegal on January 26, 1846. Although immigration records are sometimes difficult to clarify, it is believed the Twiggs family arrived in Philadelphia in the summer of 1850.

They came to Danville in August of 1856 and David Twiggs secured work in the Montour Rolling Mill working beside the puddlers. These extremely skilled workers in the iron industry had several assistants. It is not known when Mary's elderly father or her brother Samuel McClintock came to America. By 1857, they were also living in Danville in an area known as Rudy's Addition.

Mary and David Twiggs were the parents of four children, but only two, a boy of seven and a girl of ten, survived childhood to accompany the family to Danville.

A later newspaper article described Mrs. Twiggs as being of medium height, with black hair, blue eyes, a low flat forehead, coarse features, and, according to the newspaper reporter, "a tolerable fair complexion."

In Danville, as in other communities, immigrants were often crowded into subdivided homes that were probably intended for single families. Cellars, attics and make-do spaces were common. By 1857, the David Twiggs and William Clark families may have been living in the same house or, perhaps they originally lived in a double company home owned by the Montour Iron Works.

However, after David Twiggs' death several weeks earlier, Mary Twiggs would have had to move out of company housing. Perhaps the Clark family offered the Twiggs family a home or perhaps the families simply still lived close to each other. Whatever the living arrangement, when Mrs. Clark became ill, Mrs. Twiggs and Mr. Clark were her primary caregivers.

Life was hard for the men who worked in the iron mills. A puddler's job, with the help of his assistant, was described as requiring an understanding of science and the skill of an "artist." The men worked twelve-hour days, six-day weeks. On Sundays, furnaces often had to be repaired, and the men received no additional pay for that work.

For mid-century women like Mary Twiggs and Catherine Clark, managing their households required equally long hours. Tending their children, washing clothes, cleaning their homes, sewing for the family, preparing meals, and feeding their growing families on minimal wages, added to the burden of an Irish American housewife. Women tried to get along with their neighbors and extended a helping hand when they could. A person never knew when he or she – or his or her family - might need to depend upon the generosity and kindness of others.

CHAPTER 3

In Ireland, people like David and Mary Twiggs and William Clark, were very poor, but somehow they scraped together enough money to buy steerage passage to the United States. Immigrants, among them Irish, Welsh, Scotch, Germans, Lithuanians and others eked out a living in the mills and mines of Pennsylvania. Many lived in homes constructed and owned by companies like the Montour Rolling Mill, and they used scrip or vouchers to buy the necessities of life at the Company Stores.

Located in Pennsylvania's middle Susquehanna Valley, Danville was not a pretty town in the 1850s. It was smoke filled and dirty from the work at the mills and factories. On each side of Mill Street, the main thoroughfare, was a row of low, dingy, frame buildings. Some were reached by a plank from the wooden sidewalk. The street was in poor condition, and the sidewalk was only a narrow and rickety bridge resting on frail trestles of wood stuck into the mud on the level of a nearby creek. In the 1850s, there were less than a handful of brick buildings on the main street of the town.

In its "Iron Days," Danville's appearance was similar to many towns in Europe and America where the Iron Industry flourished. Rebecca Blaine Harding Davis, an eighteenth-century writer and native of Pennsylvania, wrote:

> "A cloudy day: Do you know what that is in a
> town of ironworks? The sky sank down before dawn,
> muddy, flat, immovable. The air is thick, clammy
> with the breath of crowded human beings. The
> idiosyncrasy of this town is smoke. It rolls sullenly
> in slow folds from the great chimneys of the iron-
> foundries, and settles down in black, slimy pools on
> the muddy streets."

The families of David Twiggs and William Clark were among the hundreds of thousands of immigrants who came to America in the mid-1800s. Many had to start at the bottom of the occupational ladder, taking on the dirty, smoky dangerous jobs that other workers often tried to avoid. However, employment at companies like the Montour Iron Works in Danville offered the possibilities of new beginnings and a new life for their families. They were better off than many. Although not wealthy, their lives were a marked improvement from the lives they had left behind in Ireland.

Catherine Ann Clark left Danville in mid-April of 1857 to visit her family in Philadelphia. She was nursing an infant at the time. The Clark's other child, a boy, is believed to have made the trip with her. A few days following her return to Danville on April 28, Mrs. Clark became ill. She medicated herself with magnesia, a common "tonic" that was used as a laxative. When her health wasn't improving, a neighbor administered oil and whiskey.

Mrs. Clark continued to grow worse, and a local physician, Robert S. Simington was summoned to the Clark home. His diagnosis was inflammation of the stomach and bowels, and he prescribed additional medicine to treat that ailment.

At this time, as was previously noted, the families of William Clark and Mary Twiggs may have been living in the same house and they were the primary caregivers during Mrs. Clark's illness. It was a violent one with persistent vomiting and nervous twitchings.

Catherine Ann Clark would never recover. She died on May 9. Mrs. Clark's horrific illness also sickened her nursing infant and the child died a short time later. As can happen in a small town, suspicions were aroused, and tongues were wagging among the neighbors. One woman later described mysterious conduct and intimacy between the surviving spouses after seeing Mary Twiggs place her hand on the arm of Mr. Clark while sitting with others at a table.

As has been noted, three weeks prior on April 19, and prior to Catherine Ann Clark's death, David Twiggs, Mary's husband, had died. At that time, there was no reason to suspect foul play, but when Mary Twiggs and William Clark were arrested for killing William's spouse Catherine, Coroner Elias Haas called for an inquest into Mrs. Clark's death. After their arrests, the authorities decided to exhume the body of David Twiggs. Several local physicians, William Magill, James Strawbridge, Clarence Frick, and Robert Simington, were assembled to take part in the examinations of both corpses.

Jurors empaneled for a coroner's inquest were scheduled to meet at the Montour County Courthouse on May 28. But Mrs. Twiggs wasn't feeling well and two jurors weren't present which resulted in a postponement. On June 1st, jurors were assembled and a large crowd was present to hear the evidence.

Dr. Simington testified that he had examined the stomachs of David Twiggs and Catherine Ann Clark and he declared arsenic was found in each of them. Also called to testify at the coroner's inquest were two clerks from *Chalfant and Hughes Pharmacy*, a well-respected business in the community. Thomas Chalfant, who would later become a state representative from Montour County, was a partner in the drugstore with his brother-in-law Dr. Isaac Hughes. Curtis Herrington, the first clerk to testify, said he had sold arsenic to William Clark. The second, Robert McCarty, said he had sold arsenic to Mary Twiggs.

Based on the findings of the coroner's inquest, 27-year old Mary Twiggs and 22-year-old William John Clark were immediately committed to the Montour County Jail on suspicion of murder.

However, it would be months before the prisoners would have the opportunity to tell their stories to a panel of their peers, all of whom were male.

CHAPTER 4

The jail where Mary Twiggs and William Clark were imprisoned was built in 1817. It contained two cells on the first floor and two on the second. The solid stone building also included separate living quarters for Sheriff Edward Young and his family. Twiggs and Clark were confined to the cells on the second floor.

Clark, who would testify in future court proceedings that he felt he would not receive a fair trial, devised a plan to escape. Using a piece of glass and a nail, he improvised a makeshift key that allowed him to unlock his shackles. On Saturday night, September 4, he used a piece of bone to dig a hole in a flue in the chimney inside his cell. After realizing he would not fit inside the opening, Clark began work on a second plan to gain his freedom.

When Sheriff Edward Young brought him breakfast the following morning, Clark was partially hidden behind the cell door. He violently pushed the sheriff into the cell as he was entering and then Clark quickly shut the door and bolted it.

At the same time, Mrs. Young was in a separate cell on the same floor preparing to serve breakfast to Mary Twiggs. Again, Clark acted quickly to shut Twiggs' cell door and he bolted it from the outside trapping the sheriff's wife in the cell with Mrs. Twiggs. He then grabbed the keys that Sheriff Young had left behind and ran down the stairs. He pushed aside the Sheriff's young son on the stairs as he bolted for freedom. After unlocking the outer door of the jail, Clark ran through a garden, into the alley, and headed for the Susquehanna River.

Sheriff Young immediately raised the alarm and another prisoner was able to free both Sheriff Young and his wife from their involuntary imprisonment. By this time, Clark had gotten some 300 yards across an open field, but he was quickly recaptured and taken back to the jail. He was handcuffed and his legs were securely tied to prevent any further escape attempts. A search of Clark's cell turned up a pillowcase containing his shackles and a round stone. He acknowledged the items could have been used as a weapon but insisted he did not intend to hurt anyone.

Clark admitted his ultimate plan was to wade across the river and make his way to an area known as Blue Hill. He said that after reading an August newspaper account of the hanging of David McKim for the robbery and murder of a man near Altoona, he made his decision to escape. McKim, in his final words from the gallows, said he was innocent and that witnesses had perjured themselves during his trial. Clark felt that the people of Danville were willing to swear to anything to convict him.

With his and Mary Twiggs' murder trial scheduled for September 21 in Montour County Court, Clark felt escape was his only recourse. At that time, he couldn't have known that defense attorneys were working to have the murder charges dropped against both he and Mrs. Twiggs.

CHAPTER 5

After the unsuccessful escape attempt of William Clark, his attorney Robert Clark (no relation) continued preparations to defend his client. E.H. Baldy was representing Mary Twiggs in the murder case. In September, and again in December of 1857, procedural errors were made in the selection of Grand Juries to hear the murder cases. Until the Juries presented a "true bill," the trial could not proceed.

Grand juries are reserved for serious felonies such as the murder of Catherine Clark. The panel determines if there is enough evidence to bring defendants to trial. It does not decide innocence or guilt.

Newspapers provided little information on the technicalities of the mistakes that were made, but *The Star of the North* newspaper of Bloomsburg reported in its December 30 edition that, "Owing to an unpardonable blunder committed by the Commissioners and the Sheriff, in not properly writing the Christian name, surname, occupation, and place of abode on slips of paper for drawing jurors, the array of Grand Jurors as well as Traverse Jurors, was again quashed."

On Monday December 21, the regular term of court opened in Danville, with the anticipated murder trials on the schedule. But E.H. Baldy, the attorney for Mary Twiggs surprised those present by filing a motion for dismissal of the charges and demanded freedom for the prisoners. Baldy referenced an 18th Century Act of the General Assembly which required the release of prisoners accused in felonies if they were not brought to trial within two scheduled terms of court, unless a delay had been sought by a defendant. That motion for dismissal caused quite an uproar in the community.

Judge Jordan held a hearing on the request and listened to arguments from both the defense and prosecution. Jordan turned aside the motion and the murder trial for William Clark and Mary Twiggs, beginning with the Grand Jury hearing, was then scheduled for the February 1858 term of court.

Over the winter months, while waiting for the courtroom drama to unfold, Danville residents were feeling the effects of the worst economic depression in the United States in twenty years.

In September, because there were no orders for their iron, the owners of the Montour Iron Works had to lay off all two thousand workmen and they closed the "Big Mill." In mid-October, to the credit of owners John and J.P. Grove, the workers were paid in full. The Danville Intelligencer welcomed the move, while at the same time, issuing a warning to the laid off workers. "Now let the men be careful of their money---and we may go through this winter with but little trouble."

But high food prices continued to place hardships on the residents, leading one pundit to say that not only was the price of eggs higher, but the eggs were smaller. Several meetings were held by community leaders to come up with ideas to alleviate the food shortages. These included construction of a local Market House and a flour exchange and purchasing food in nearby towns to help feed the families impacted by the work stoppage at the Montour Iron Works. However, inaction by those appointed to come up with resolutions to the problems and economic turmoil ended with no clear answers.

CHAPTER 6

As the February term of Court opened in Montour County, attorneys for Mary Twiggs and William Clark asked that the defendants be tried separately. Judge Alexander Jordan agreed to the request. William Clark's attorney Robert F. Clark then filed several motions on behalf of his client.

The defense attorney contended that the court had erred when it refused to release William Clark from jail in December. Attorney Robert Clark maintained he had not been tried within the time spelled out in the law. Attorney Clark also attempted to quash the Grand Jury at the Court proceedings opening on February 16. The attorney challenged the selection of Matthew S. Ridgway, whose occupation was listed as a Mill Boss saying that description was not one recognized under the law. Also questioned was whether presiding Judge Alexander Jordan had the authority to oversee the trial. It was argued that Jordan had not been elected to represent Montour County in the judicial district, and should, therefore, not be the one to hear the case. Judge Jordan dismissed the challenges. An immediate appeal was filed with the Pennsylvania Supreme Court on behalf of William Clark.

Before actual testimony at trial could begin during the regular term of court, Judge Jordan spoke to the men assembled as a Grand Jury. That panel had to determine whether prosecutors had gathered enough evidence to actually hold the murder suspects for trial. Within a short period of time, the Grand Jury retired, examined the prosecution's evidence and returned with a True Bill against William John Clark and Mary Twiggs for the murder of Catherine Ann Clark.

A jury was then empaneled from throughout Montour County to hear the evidence that had been gathered by both prosecutors and defense attorneys for Clark's trial.

As testimony opened on February 16, 1858, Dr. Robert Simington, the attending physician for Catherine Ann Clark, was the first to take the witness stand. Simington said when he first attended the woman, she appeared extremely exhausted and he prescribed medicine for what he diagnosed as inflammation of the bowels and stomach. The doctor said he returned to the Clark home when Mrs. Clark's condition worsened. He testified that William Clark and Mary Twiggs told him they had administered magnesia purchased at the Company Store. Simington testified he did not personally examine the medicine being administered. Simington told the court that, based on his examination, Mrs. Clark died from arsenic poisoning. According to the doctor, a post-mortem of her body found white particles in the woman's stomach that tested positive for arsenic.

Dr. James Strawbridge corroborated Simington's testimony, saying his examination of the stomach's contents proved that no other substance would have produced the appearances they had found and that the tests proved positive for arsenic.

Doctors Frick, Magill and Snitzler, who had also been present at the postmortem, agreed. It should be noted that arsenic was considered the "poison of kings" and, at this time in history, was a "popular" murder weapon. History is riddled with accounts of both royalty and commoners carrying out assassinations for personal gain using the odorless, tasteless compounds of arsenic.

Among those taking the stand for the Commonwealth in the afternoon were Curtis Herrington, and Robert McCarty. Also testifying were neighbors of David and Mary Twiggs, Jane Harris, Jane Dougherty, Mary Richard, Barbara Desinger, Dennis and Mary Egan, Catharine Palhemus and Isaac Gulick.Their testimony, centered on the alleged "trifling familiarity" between Mrs. Twiggs and William Clark.

Curtis Herrington, a clerk at the drugstore of *Chalfant and Hughes*, testified that he knew Clark by sight and had sold him an ounce of arsenic in March and another in April. He stated that Clark told him he needed the arsenic to kill rats.

On two other occasions, Herrington said, he sold Clark strychnine, and in early May sold him magnesia and more arsenic.

Among other witnesses called to testify was a neighbor, Charlotte McMullen. She stated she lived a block from the Clark home and was acquainted with the family. Her husband Daniel was also an iron puddler in the Big Mill. Mrs. McMullen was similar in age to Mrs. Clark and was the mother of at least one child who was born in April. The Twiggs' and Clarks' along with many of the Irish families lived in in the same neighborhood in Danville. At that time, the town was divided into a North Ward and a South Ward. In 1867, Danville was further divided into four wards and the area in which many of the Irish families lived became known as the "Bloody Third." It was known as a rough section of town, where the men worked hard, drank hard, and often fought hard during a night on the town.

Mrs. McMullen testified she saw Mrs. Clark the day she returned from Philadelphia and the woman appeared fine. She also said she saw Mrs. Clark a few days later when she was ill. Mrs. Clark was complaining of stomach pain and said her husband and Mrs. Twiggs had been caring for her. On cross examination, Mrs. McMullen said she visited Mrs. Clark during the illness and brought her oil in whiskey and tea to the home. She said other women were also present during some of her frequent visits.

Mrs. McMullen added that in Mrs. Clark's presence she told Mr. Clark that rumors were circulating in the neighborhood that he had poisoned his wife. When asked who was circulating the rumors, Mrs. McMullen said it was "a flying report all over." According to Mrs. McMullen's testimony, Clark said he would take care of the report after his wife was buried. Mrs. McMullen also told the court she asked Mrs. Clark directly if she felt she had been poisoned by her husband and Mrs. Clark said "no."

One of the most damning pieces of evidence during William Clark's trial was a letter that was supposedly written by Clark on August 29, 1857, to a friend, Andrew Thompson, who lived in Phoenixville. Thompson and a man named John Stewart had visited Clark shortly after he was jailed the previous May. Prosecutors had Thompson take the witness stand and describe the contents of the letter he received from Clark the previous summer.

According to Thompson, the letter asked him to buy the exact amounts of arsenic and strychnine that Clark had purchased, according to testimony, in Danville. The letter asked Thompson to visit Clark at the jail in early September – along with Clark's attorney - and slip him the items when the attorney wasn't looking.

However, Thompson turned the letter over to the authorities and it was put into evidence at Clark's trial. No one seems to have asked why William Clark would have wanted the exact amounts of arsenic that the clerk had testified Clark purchased.

Others called to the witness stand included Jane Harris, Dennis and Mary Egan, and H. Waugh. All testified to Clark's frequent visits to the Twiggs' home and what they described as excessive familiarity between Clark and Mrs. Twiggs.

Mary Twiggs' father Mr. McClintock who lived with her, testified that he never saw Clark at their house later than 10 o'clock at night; never saw anything improper between him and Mrs. Twiggs; and, he added, that his daughter and Mrs. Egan, one of the earlier witnesses, were not good friends.

One of those testifying on behalf of Clark was Dennis Emery who may have been a co-worker. He told the court that David Twiggs was Clark's helper at the iron mill and they appeared to be good friends. Mr. Emery described William Clark as industrious, peaceful, and affectionate to his wife.

Thompson Foster also testified to Clark's good character and said he never saw anything improper between him and Mrs. Twiggs. Foster accompanied Clark after his wife's death to the office of Dr. Simington for the examination of her body. However, Dr. Simington was not in his office at the time.

Trial testimony ended on Thursday afternoon when attorney Paul Leidy summed up the Commonwealth's case. His presentation was followed by William Clark's attorney, Robert F. Clark. The *Columbia Democrat Newspaper* described the two hours of rebuttal as both eloquent and professional. According to the story, attorney Clark "manfully battled against the fearful weight of the testimony" and "no appeals how fervent could stem the tide against the prisoner."

On Friday morning, William G Hurley, another of Clark's attorneys, presented a final summation to the jury. His presentation was followed by J. W. Comly who closed the case for the Commonwealth.

Judge Alex Jordan then addressed the jury and laid out the facts and circumstances presented by the various witnesses during the trial. He asked the jurors to consider a motive for the death of Mrs. Clark. The judge said there was no direct proof that William Clark administered poison to his wife, but direct proof is not required for a conviction. He added, however, that the law did require such proof as fixes guilt upon the accused beyond all reasonable doubt.

Jordan reminded the jury of the letter Clark sent to a friend, asking him to buy and deliver exact quantities of arsenic and strychnine and bring them to his jail cell. Regarding Clark's failed escape from prison, Judge Jordan said while guilt may have been inferred by the attempt, circumstances were insufficient to justify a conviction.

The judge also reminded the jury of trial testimony in which defense attorney Robert Clark asked Thompson Foster and Samuel McClintock, the brother of Mary Twiggs, about alleged rumors that Mrs. Clark had been poisoned. Clark's friend, Thompson Foster, said Clark wanted to have Dr. Robert Simington examine his wife's body to prove that poisoning was not her cause of death. The judge told jurors to ask themselves why, if the prisoner did administer poison to his wife or knew that it had been administered to her by his procurement and with his knowledge, he would have desired an examination to be made that might lead to his detection.

Jordan reflected on testimony regarding Clark's good character prior to the death of his wife, which could also be relied upon as grounds for his acquittal. He added, however, that when guilt is fixed upon an individual, previous good conduct cannot wipe it out.

In conclusion, Judge Jordan said if the jury was satisfied of Clark's guilt, they needed to convict him. If not, he needed to be acquitted.

At one o'clock on February 18, 1858, the jurors retired to begin deliberations.

Six hours later, at 7 p.m., the bell in the courthouse tower rang indicating that the jury had reached a verdict in the most infamous trial held in Montour County.

Within minutes a crowd spilled into the courtroom to await the decision. One local newspaper described William Clark's demeanor as downcast and trembling as he was brought into the courtroom.

However, he appeared to listen with a degree of composure as every juror was polled and pronounced the word "guilty." Judge Jordan immediately adjourned the trial until Saturday morning.

CHAPTER 7

The courtroom was packed to overflowing as Judge Alex Jordan reconvened court at 8:30 a.m. on Saturday, February 20, 1858. The Judge asked William Clark if he had anything to say as to why the sentence of death should not be imposed against him.

In a clear voice, William Clark addressed the Courtroom.

> I do not object that the sentence of death shall now be pronounced upon me—I am prepared to die. Innocence of the foul crime charged upon me has strengthened me during the long confinement and during the trial and is serving me now in this awful hour.
>
> I do not wish to charge the jury, or the Court with unfairness, but God, the judge of judges, the ruler of princes, who searches the heart and knows the inmost workings of it is my judge, and I am prepared and satisfied to go into his presence. It makes no difference how a man dies, if he is prepared, only so he don't kill himself. The other deaths he need not fear. Man only can kill the body, but God can kill body and soul. I stand here before God and this large audience an innocent man. I know it is a painful duty to you to pass the sentence of death upon me, and I don't envy your Honor to pass that sentence, for the law requires it.
>
> But since God has strengthened me to bear the trial with fortitude he will do (so) now, and I feel satisfied to enter into eternity. It is no use of me to comment upon my innocence, but I declare it again in the presence of this assemblage, the Court, and Almighty God, who sees and hears everything, and who is to be my Judge, and knows that I am not

guilty of the felonious crime of murdering my own wife. But, as I said before, to comment upon my innocence is useless in such a prejudiced community as this.

When at the last Court, application was made for my discharge on a point of law, the public feeling was so strong against me, that they cried out that if your Honor did so, they would kill me. And it is, therefore, that I don't blame you for refusing to discharge me then and giving your own body to the public. I decline to comment upon the trial at this time--those who have injured me I leave to God who will judge correctly and justly. I don't want to comment upon them: but what shall the jury and those who testified against me think hereafter, when the truth may come out, for thus having accused me without cause and wrongfully.

Here are the lips (pointing to his lips) that were never polluted by a harlot's kiss, and here is a breast (pointing to his breast) on which a prostitute never reposed, and here is the heart (pointing to his heart) that never beat for a strange woman, and I am innocent of the foul charge. I have nothing more to say now. You can proceed to pass sentence."

Judge Jordan looked squarely at Clark and proceeded to carry out his duty.

I did hope that during my official term, I would have been spared the pain of passing upon anyone the awful sentence of death. This hope, like many others in which I have fondly indulged, has vanished. The duty of the law imposed upon the Court, is a most solemn and painful one; but it must be discharged.

The crime for which you have been convicted by a jury of your country, is the murder of your wife under circumstances, which if possible, aggravate the enormity of the crime, and impart to it a deeper and darker stain, than is usually found in cases of murder. Catherine Ann Clark was your wife, and from the evidence in the case, was not wanting in duty and affection for you. It is but a few years since she gave you her heart and merged her name in yours--since you mutually promised at the marriage altar, to support, love, comfort and cherish each other, in sickness and in health, so long as God permitted you to live together.

From the evidence, it appears that you lived together happily. She was the mother of your children. It was an evil hour for you, when forgetting your duty to her, your duty to your God and to your country, you administered to her a deadly potion that soon terminated her life. She did not suspect that when you were in her sickroom, and stood by her, day after day apparently anxious for her recovery, that the cup you presented to her contained a deadly potion, and that you were seeking to destroy her life. She did not suspect that the agonies she was suffering in the pains she was enduring were caused by you. Oh, it was a deed of the foulest kind, evincing a hardness of heart that has scarcely a parallel.

Your guilt, which is established by the verdict in this case would in all probability not have been detected, had it not been for the examination made by the physicians after her death. In her stomach was found the evidence of the cause of her death. During the brief period that may elapse between this and the time when the sentence of the law may be executed, the Court would most solemnly and earnestly urge upon you, the duty of endeavoring to prepare to meet a Judge from whose dread sentence there is no appeal, from whose eye no one can escape, and who is able, with unerring certainty to distinguish between the innocent and the guilty. Do not neglect this with hope that the Executive clemency will spare you.

The Court most deeply sympathizes with you, but our sympathies cannot prevent the sentence of death or its execution. You have had the benefit of a fair trial—you have been defended, and ably defended by your counsel and you have been condemned by a jury of your country. It remains for the Court to pass upon the sentence of the law, and that is that you William John Clark, be taken hence, to the place where whence you came, within the jail of the County of Montour, and from thence to the place of execution, within the walls or yard of the said jail, and that you be there hanged by the neck until you are dead. And may God have mercy upon your soul.

CHAPTER 8

In early May of 1858, Pennsylvania's Supreme Court heard the appeal of William J. Clark who alleged several errors were made during his February trial. However, without delay, Chief Justice George W. Woodward sustained the ruling of Judge Alex Jordan.

That decision came down as the murder trial of Mary Twiggs got underway in Montour County on Monday, May 17, 1858, at the Montour County Courthouse in Danville. According to the *Danville Intelligencer* newspaper, "The anticipated trial of Mrs. Twiggs, for the murder of Mrs. Clark, brought many strangers to town. As was the case for the William Clark trial, the ringing of the bell at 2 p.m. soon filled the courtroom with witnesses, jurors and spectators."

Mary Twiggs entered the court room and was seated between her defense attorneys, Edward Baldy and Robert Clark. Her brother, Samuel McClintock sat to Baldy's right. Judge Jordan told Mrs. Twiggs that during the selection of the jury she was entitled to 20 preemptory challenges. Challenges allow attorneys to veto potential jurors. Approximately six of every seven of the prospective jurors were challenged by the woman's legal team as having already formed an opinion on her innocence or guilt.

By the time eighty men had been interviewed to serve on the jury, only eleven had been selected, and the pool of candidates was exhausted. Augustus George, James Bryson, George Cotner, John Moyer, John Cromley, Sr, Benjamin Diefenbacher, Peter Handshaw, John Vought Jr, Samuel Muffley, John McGonigal, and Daniel Carey were sworn in as Jurors. Judge Alex Jordan then asked Sheriff Edward Young to summon 30 additional potential jurors from Montour County and to order them to appear Tuesday morning at eight o'clock.

The following morning, after a number of additional challenges, John Rank was accepted and sworn as the 12th juror. B. K. Rhodes, the prosecuting attorney then called the first witnesses. Doctors Simington, McGill, Strawbridge and Frick along with Charlotte McMullen were called as witnesses for the prosecution. The testimony of the physicians was, in substance, the same they had offered during the Clark trial. Mrs. McMullen testified that she lived a block from the Twiggs and the Clarks. The rest of her testimony repeated what she had said at Clark's trial.

Court then adjourned until 2:00 p.m.

Among those taking the stand for the Commonwealth in the afternoon were Curtis Herrington, and Robert McCarty, clerks at the Danville drugstore of *Chalfant and Hughes*. Also testifying were neighbors of David and Mary Twiggs: Jane Harris, Jane Dougherty, Mary Richard, Barbara Desinger, Dennis and Mary Egan, Catharine Palhemus and Isaac Gulick. Their testimony centered on the alleged "trifling familiarity" between Mrs. Twiggs and William Clark.

Other witnesses who had testified at the coroner's inquest and Clark's trial presented similar testimony. The exception was that of drugstore clerk Robert McCarty who suffered intense cross examination at the hands of Attorney Baldy and seemed to contradict his previous testimony.

William Stahl, a new witness testified that he had seen Mrs. Twiggs and Mr. Clark sitting along the creek one morning at four o'clock. Stahl said Clark had his arm around her neck. Peter Foley, who was with Stahl said he was positive of their identity although he had not seen them together on other occasions.

At that point, the prosecution ended its case. Edward Baldy then opened for the defense before the trial was adjourned until the following morning.

On Wednesday morning, defense witnesses included William McClintock, the aged father of Mary Twiggs, and her brother Samuel. Other defense witnesses included Thompson Foster, John McClugan, William Henrie, Samuel Stroh, Cornelius Garretson, James Hughes, and Pat Daugherty. Presumably, these witnesses testified to Mary Twiggs good character and their belief she could not commit murder.

After the defense concluded its case, prosecuting attorney B.K. Rhodes spent an hour in presenting the prosecution's closing arguments. At the conclusion of his presentation, court was adjourned for a lunch break.

When court reconvened at two o'clock in the afternoon, E.H. Baldy, Mary Twiggs' attorney, spent two hours and 20 minutes in his closing summation. He accused some of the Commonwealth witnesses of displaying open animosity toward his client.

Mrs. Twiggs frequently brushed tears from her eyes as the trial drew to a close. Finally, another Commonwealth attorney, Joshua W. Cromly, spent more than an hour and a half addressing jurors. One newspaper called his speech "a rare combination of biting sarcasm, impassioned eloquence, and telling logic."

Judge Jordan used thirty-five minutes in his charge to the jury before it retired at 6:30 Wednesday evening. Mrs. Twiggs was returned to her jail cell to await the verdict.

Newspaper accounts reported that during the jury's deliberations the next day, Thursday, the jurors were split on the first ballot. Two of the twelve jurors voted for the acquittal of Mrs. Twiggs. However, at two o'clock that afternoon, the panel returned with a verdict of "guilty."

Defense attorney E.H. Baldy immediately called for a new trial on the grounds that one of the jurors had expressed his opinion of guilt before entering the jury box. Several witnesses testified that they had heard one of the jurors, John Cromley, declare that previous to the trial he believed Mary Twiggs was guilty. Cromley was then sworn by the judge and questioned. He denied the charge and the court was adjourned until the following morning.

On Friday morning May 21, 1858, spectators crowded the courtroom and heard Judge Jordan dismiss defense arguments for a new trial. He then turned to Mary Twiggs and asked her to rise. When the judge asked her if she had anything to say as to why the sentence of death should not be imposed against her, she did not offer a reply.

Judge Jordan then addressed the convicted woman.

> "Mary Twiggs, a jury of your country have found you guilty of the murder of Catherine Ann Clark, and it now becomes my duty to pronounce upon you the sentence of death. I refrain from making any remarks that might tend to increase your sorrows or deepen the anguish you must now feel. To the court, this trial and issue have been most painful. We have endeavored to give you a fair trial and afforded you

every opportunity to establish your innocence if you could. We gave you at the trial the full benefit of all the legal positions taken by your faithful and able counsel; the jury have, after many hours of calm and serious deliberation, declared their belief in your guilt. If you have been unjustly condemned, it has not been because those whose duty it was to pass upon your guilt or innocence, desired your condemnation.

The weight of evidence, they believed, was against you, and demanded from them a verdict of guilty. The Court would most earnestly recommend and entreat of you to spend the brief time there probably is, between you and eternity, in preparing to meet your final Judge. To Him, your guilt or innocence is well-known.

"The sentence of the Court is, that you, Mary Twiggs, be taken hence to the place from whence you came, within the jail of the County of Montour, and from thence to the place of execution, within the walls or yard of the said jail, and that you there be hanged by the neck until you are dead, and may God have mercy on your soul.

CHAPTER 9

On July 8, 1858, William Packer, Governor of Pennsylvania, signed execution orders establishing the dates William J. Clark and Mary Twiggs would be hanged.

Clark's execution was scheduled for September 24, 1858. After hearing the Sheriff read the order to him, he asked Sheriff Young for a pipe of tobacco.

Mrs. Twiggs was visibly shaken when Montour County Sheriff Edward Young read the order for execution to her in her jail cell. October 22, 1858 was the date set for the hanging of Mary Twiggs.

Also in July, Clark issued a lengthy statement that was published in local newspapers proclaiming his innocence and blaming others for his conviction. His letter was filled with Biblical passages and perspective, indicating more than just a passing knowledge of the church in which he had been a congregant. *The Sunbury Gazette* carried a portion of Clark's letter in its July 31, 1858 edition.

> The reason I make this statement is first because I pity those who have been mistaken by false evidence to condemn the innocent. Secondly, because I believe the many Christians - servants of God and friends of justice - throughout Montour and other counties who are obliged to hold me legally guilty, and demand the punishment incurred while I am innocent.
>
> Thirdly, because I want to present all the leading points in each deponents testimony, and inform you what is true and what is not true; that I may feel and know that I have done my whole duty to the Commonwealth, to society, to God my next judge, and to my own soul.
>
> Fourthly and finally, to show that I maintain my innocence and stand acquitted in the presence of the

all omnipresent God, who has made the ear and can hear, who has made the eye and can see; whilst I stand condemned before my fellow man; that my many friends and relatives may have faith in me, having part in the first resurrection through Christ: for every false accusation will add a new gem to the diadem that is prepared for me, the innocent victim of persecution.

Clark's detailed proclamation of his innocence took aim at the court testimony of Curtis Herrington. The clerk at the Danville drug store of *Chalfant and Hughes* had told the court he sold Clark arsenic and strychnine.

First. Justice, as well as you and I were imposed on by the mistaken testimony of Curtis Herrington,whether intentionally or unintentionally, I cannot tell; but, we shall all know which it was at the judgment seat of Christ. This is the substance of his testimony: I sold Clark 2 1/2 ounces of arsenic and eight grains of strychnine, in about five or six weeks' time, and told Clark that if the 2 1/2 ounces of arsenic did not answer the purpose he should come again and I would give him something stronger. Herrington said, "I did not know his name; I kept no register; I sold arsenic to others, whom I thought proper persons; I first learned Clark's name after he was arrested; I did not know where he lived."

In rebutting Herrington's testimony, Clark said,

Now if Curtis Herrington had kept a register he would have had the date and the name of him to whom he sold that amount, if he had sold it to any individual. How could he think a man whose name he did not know a proper person? How could he invite such a man to come again and get stronger poison, if for a hundred 60 grains of arsenic did not answer? I say how could he invite him back without getting his address? Did he think such a person a proper person to sell poison in wholesale form?

Again if he felt justified in giving his testimony, he would have made mention of the parts of the days in which he swears he sold it. That would have given justice an opportunity to judge the truth or falsity of his testimony to prove where I had been in them parts of days, and thereby showing that I did not purchase it.
This indefinite testimony left me either to lie or tell the truth and contradict him. I chose the latter and declared the truth, that I never purchased poison of any kind, nor ever sought any kind of poison to my knowing or knowledge. I now again reiterate the same, and shalt seal it with my dying breath.

I wish to call your attention a little further to the real nature of his testimony, that you may apply your reason. The table of small weights, or druggists table of small weights, as appears in the arithmetic shows as follows: 20 grams one scruple, 20 scruples one drachm, 8 drachms one ounce, 12 ounces one pound; 2 1/2 ounces making 1200 grains. Medical theory informs us that three grains of arsenic will destroy the life of a healthy individual, and that half a grain of strychnine will do the same. Now we see that 2 ½ ounces of arsenic and eight grains of strychnine will destroy the lives of 460 persons, by the report of the medical theory.

Curtis Herrington swears that he sold all that to one person to kill rats, enough to kill all the rats in Pennsylvania. I question whether druggists sell poisons without receiving a pledge from the purchaser.

In his proclamation, the condemned killer offered an explanation surrounding the letter which the prosecution said he wrote to a friend, Andrew Thompson, at Phoenixville. The letter asked Thompson to purchase poison in the exact amounts he had "supposedly" purchased and bring it to his cell at Danville. Clark said he never wrote that letter, contending that it was the work of his enemies.

> Mr. Editor, I would present to your many readers, several persons, by name, who was malignant enough to devise and form that trap for my destruction. But I feel that I have said enough on this point to convince any honest mind that that letter was written by a secret enemy of mine. Because I attended eminence over all that resided by where I did, they hated me. Because I manifested an independent and fearless spirit amongst the papist tribe, they conspired to destroy me. Because I was a member of a society and a member of a secret order, which popery, personally, collectively and eternally hates, they were not satisfied with destroying me, but they endeavored to cast suspicion on said order.

In explaining his attempted prison escape Clark said, based on what he had heard and seen, he knew he was going to be condemned unjustly, and he asked himself, *"Shall I suffer an ignominious death without attempting to escape? The apostle Peter escaped out of prison when unjustly confined, and so will I."*

As he continued to press his claims of innocence, Clark maintained that while on her deathbed, his wife had also declared his innocence.

> Here is another fact, sufficient of itself, standing alone, to prove that I am innocent, and that is the dying declaration of my wife. When asked by Charlotte McMullen, "Did your husband, William J. Clark, poison you?" "No, never!" "Then did Mrs. Twiggs give you anything to hurt you?" "No, never."

That is the correct questions of Mrs. McMullen, and the correct answers of Catherine Ann Clark.

Reader, what does law define the dying declaration of the man or woman to be? Why law defines it to be direct and positive. How many have been condemned by the declaration of the dying? And here is William J. Clark condemned, in a dying declaration protesting his (or my) innocence. "Did William J. Clark poison you?" "No never." "Did Mrs. Twiggs give you anything to hurt you?" "No never." Is that not direct and positive proof that I am innocent?

There are only two inferences (that) can be legitimately drawn from the words "no, "never" and each inference proves that I am innocent. When asked if she was poisoned she did not say "No never" but when asked if I poisoned her she said "No never. And did Mrs. Twiggs give you anything to hurt you? "No."

Clark then closed out his statement of innocence.

If there was five times the amount of false testimony given against me, no jury is justified in condemning me while there was such strong and positive evidence of my innocence. Can I accuse the administration of law with injustice in as much as I am unjustly condemned? No, by no means, for the administration of the law's grand motto is "Justice"; and his Honor explained the necessary points of law impartially.

Am I to accuse law? No, by no means, for law is justice, and the strict adherence to law is justice. Law is the regulator of rights. Law is the mainspring of all domestic prosperity. Law is the driving wheel of this glorious Republic, this basis of the globe, this free Constitution, this asylum for the refugees of foreign despotism: and without this glorious institution of law and the strict adherence to the same, this paradise on earth would soon become a barren waste, a field of woe, a whited sepulcher.

But I accuse false witnesses and secret enemies for manufacturing and swearing against me false testimonies.

Abominable and absurd as they are, they are not able to destroy the evidence of my innocence. Therefore I do not say they are wholly my judicial murderers, though they made a bold attempt to be, and they shall bear a part, for "Thou shalt not bear false witness against thy neighbor."

And I accuse the jury of ignorance and stupidity, for not adhering strictly to the law, for the law says in no place to condemn the innocent when there is evidence consistent with the innocence of the accused. I forgive any who have wronged me unintentionally, and I hope God will forgive them. And all who have intentionally taken a part against me unjustly and become my judicial murderers

I leave to God, whose high prerogative is to make inquisition. Any of the jury who reads this, I want them to open wide the napkin that contains their intellect for they will not need their hearing faculties. And any of the witnesses who may grumble at this, I would say that I care not what they say.

If a Jesuit, a papist makes any fuss or grumbles about it, I say I am not surprised at anything they will do or say against me; and if anyone will say that this prejudices him still more against me, I would say to him that if he is anxious to see me unjustly murdered on the scaffold, I do not want his sympathy; and if any should find objection to the spirit in which I have written, I would point him to the answer of Job went accused of resumption by Bildad (one of Job's three comforters) for maintaining his innocence.

Said Job, "Why do you persecute me as God, and are not satisfied with my flesh?" Again, in the words of Paul, an apostle of our Lord Jesus Christ, the true vine, of whom I claim to be a branch, as written in the second book of Timothy, fourth chapter 14th verse, and if any profess to be a judge of my soul on earth, I want him to read the 1st and 2nd verses of the seventh chapter of St. Matthew.

I also forewarn all teachers, spiritual pastors and masters, professors and mechanics of every kind, rich and poor, male and female, who may come to visit me, to remain neutral on the subject of my condemnation or execution: if they cannot believe me innocent; for I shall not listen to any more insinuations on the subject. And if any have a desire to start me on the question, I invite them to commit their thoughts to paper, with their proper address and hand them in, and I will probably answer them through this medium.

Reader, I have come nigh to close and I feel that I have done my duty by explaining the case as I know it, that you may know when my worthless body may be with its mother dust, that my judicial murderers are cherished in the bosom of the community, and I feel confident that every impartial, just man, of common sense and reason, can see that my secret enemies have taken advantage of my helplessness, and made the law a cloak for their crime, and that the

jury either through stupidity or morbidness did not
adhere to the requirements of law and justice."

Montour American newspaper editor D.H. B. Brower offered
readers William Clark's full statement in a pamphlet for 10 cents at
the time of its publication.

CHAPTER 10

During the last weekend in July, William Clark's brother, Alexander visited the condemned prisoner in the Montour County Jail. The *Danville Intelligencer* reported they discussed arrangements for the disposition of Clark's body following his execution.

He also asked his brother to visit him on September 24, the day he was scheduled for the gallows. The newspaper wrote that Alexander declined the request, considering the emotional impact he was being asked to bear. Sheriff Edward Young said Clark showed no emotion as he and his brother said goodbye for the final time. Sheriff Young revealed that the only time he had seen any tears from the convicted killer came when he handed Young two books for his son who was in Alexander's care.

In the first weeks of September, a local carpenter, Charles Diehl completed the construction of the gallows at a local planing mill (a place where lumber is finished) and tested its worthiness before it was reconstructed in the prison yard.

At the jail, one of the persons who came to see Clark was drug store clerk Curtis Herrington who had told a packed court room that he sold Clark the strychnine and arsenic used to poison his wife.

Clark vehemently denied the claim during his declaration of innocence, questioning Herrington's credibility. Clark refused to talk, shake hands, or look at Herrington during the visit to his cell.

September 24, the day of Clark's execution, was overcast and rainy. Although the actual hanging was to be closed to the public, curiosity drew both men and women to the jail yard in the morning hours to watch the reconstruction of the gallows. Also on display was the coffin awaiting Clark's remains, which was the work of Augustus Arms.

Eventually the crowd was ushered out of the jail yard and into the streets by sheriff "deputies" who wore printed badges and had been sworn specifically for that day. As the crowd continued to build outside the prison walls, two military units, the Columbia Guards and the Montour Rifles were also on hand to maintain order.

As required by law, Sheriff Young had assembled a Jury to witness the execution. That panel of observers, along with ministers, physicians, deputies and reporters, were the only people allowed inside the prison yard.

During his confinement, Clark was frequently visited by several ministers from churches in the community. Not only did they try to supply his spiritual needs, they pressed him to make a full confession to killing his wife and David Twiggs. But he continued to deny having any part in the deaths.

Two men from Danville, Peter Harder and George Souder, volunteered to spend the night with Clark before his execution. They read various passages of Scripture. He told the men repeatedly that death had no sting for him, that he was at peace with his God, and that he had for the last three weeks suffered not the slightest fear of dying.

Clark said he had nothing to regret, he hoped to see them in another and better world and that he died with no ill feelings toward anyone.

For some unknown reason Clark burned a number of papers which he had written and went to sleep a little after midnight. He rested quietly and slept soundly for several hours.

Before Harder and Souder left in the morning, he prayed with the men, and appeared solemn and earnest as he awaited his fate.

For breakfast he had some bread, water, brandy and sugar, commonly called "panada." After that, he smoked a cigar, wrote out his speech to be delivered on the gallows, and calmly spoke with several visitors.

Between 9 and 10 a.m., several ministers entered his cell. The Reverend Dr. J. W. Yeomans led them in a fervent prayer. At 11 o'clock, the prisoner was brought to the scaffold. He was linked arm in arm with the Sheriff and the Reverend Mr. Hall, the local Baptist preacher. They were followed by the Reverends Stover, Harder, Yeomans, Crampton and Oppenheimer.

William Clark climbed the stairs to the gallows with a firm and unfaltering step. For forty-five minutes or so, Clark read his prepared remarks. He said that he was not guilty of the crimes for which he was convicted. He stated that Curtis Herrington and another witness, Mrs. Harris, had lied during his trial. Clark denied having bought poison and said that Robert McCarty, who worked at the same drug store with Herrington, realized his mistake and recanted his initial statements to authorities. Clark also contended that Judge Alexander Jordan was influenced by false evidence and had sentenced him unjustly.

When the coffin was brought before the scaffold, Clark's voice faltered and trembled. At one point during his statement, he requested that Dr. Robert Simington come onto the platform and give him a drink. He continued to drink water throughout the course of his speech.

As to the guilt or innocence of Mary Twiggs, William Clark believed she was innocent and, although she had the opportunity to administer poison to his wife, he could not see any motive as to why she would do so. Clark said that he never saw anyone giving his wife poison or knowing anything about it --- that his wife refused to take a cup of water from a neighbor, Mrs. Mullen, an hour before her death.

He said he could throw no light on the death of David Twiggs, other than that Mrs. McMullen made punch for Twiggs, and a short time after he drank it, he began vomiting and continued to do so until he died.

He said he did not know what was in the punch. Among his last words, "I never purchased poison to the best of my knowledge. In my death I go where my heaven will be more glorious. I am innocent, glory be to God."

He thanked his attorneys and ministers for their faithfulness, and also the Danville newspaper editors for not prejudicing his case before the trial. He then said his goodbyes to his friends and relatives, although they were not present. William Clark, the condemned man, also thanked Dr. Simington and Sheriff Young.

Clark finished his speech shortly before noon. The Reverend Mr. Stover then read the tenth chapter of Job followed by a prayer from the Reverend Mr. Hall at which time the prisoner knelt in prayer.

Also at Clark's request, the Reverend Mr. Harden sang the hymn, "Rock of Ages." Clark joined in with the singing.

The black cap was then drawn over William Clark's head by the Sheriff and his arms were pinioned behind him. After descending the gallows, the Sheriff called out, "William J. Clark, do you still live."

The prisoner answered in a firm voice "I live!"

The drop fell immediately, and William J. Clark was launched into eternity at six minutes after twelve o'clock on September 24, 1858. Thirty minutes later, his body was brought down from the gallows, and he was pronounced dead by Drs. Simington, Magill and Strawbridge.

William Clark's body was then placed in the coffin and taken to the front of the jail on Market Street. At that time, the crowd was given the opportunity to view it. The body was buried that afternoon at the poor house farm, a few miles east of Danville.

CHAPTER 11

Four days after the execution of William Clark, Mary Twiggs attempted to escape from her prison cell. Twiggs was well aware of the details surrounding the execution of Clark in the jail yard below her cell and perhaps she thought it was her best chance of escaping the hangman.

Using a small nail and a chicken bone, about four or five inches in length, she tried to create a hole in the wall of her cell. After feigning an illness, Twiggs aroused the suspicions of Sheriff Young.

A search of the cell found a large quantity of dirt under her bed and several larger stones still loosely embedded in the wall. As a result, she was handcuffed and placed in the cell that once held Clark.

There is no daily log of the people who visited Mary Twiggs during her time in prison. As mentioned previously, she was an Irish Protestant and a member of the Presbyterian Church.

One of the spiritual advisers during her long confinement, was the Reverend Dr. John W. Yeomans, a well-known and highly respected minister in Danville who had accompanied Clark to his execution. He kept notes of his conversations with Mrs. Twiggs beginning on the day following her escape attempt.

"You have been trying to break out," Yeomans commented.

"I have indeed," said Mrs. Twiggs. "I did want to get out so bad. I heard some of the sheriff's folks saying in the yard, they were going to put me into Clark's room, and I thought it dreadful."

Yeomans then asked, "But how could you hope to get away, a woman as you are, if you had got out? You must know they would certainly catch you!"

Mrs. Twiggs offered this response. "I know. But perhaps they wouldn't care to catch a poor desolate woman if she once got out. There are some that don't feel so bad against me, and if they once did see me out, would let me go."

She continued, "I heard that Judge Moore had said he didn't think I ought to have been convicted on that boy's testimony that I bought the poison. He (Moore) is a good and kind man they tell me, and he has charge of that place (the poor house) where my old father is, and my child. I thought if I could get there, he would let me stay there a while till I could get away. But I didn't know, and indeed I didn't think it any matter what became of me, if I could get away. For I would rather die anywhere or anyway you know, where Goodness should will it, then to die innocent on the gallows here."

Mrs. Twiggs added, "Oh you know sir, I didn't think much how it would go with me when I got out. But I thought if my Heavenly Father would help me to get out, it would be a mercy. And he would lead me somehow after."

Yeomans replied, "I'm sorry you did that. It will make it harder to do anything for you, if any were disposed you are innocent."

"Think it will?" she asked. "It's no sign I'm guilty. I shouldn't try, nor wish to get out if I hadn't been innocent. I would be perfectly willing to suffer this terrible death if I were guilty. But Satan has put me in here by using some people that were prejudiced."

But Reverend Yeomans countered, "I'm afraid you don't tell me the truth. Clark has gone out of this world denying the truth I fear, and if he has it is a dreadful thing for him. And if you do the same it will be dreadful for you."

"I don't know anything at all about Clark, whether he is guilty or innocent" she said. "I never knew anything bad about him, as if he would poison his wife or my husband. I did not like him altogether, not that I saw anything very ill about him, but he was light and trifling like, many times and acted foolish."

Yeomans then asked her a pointed question, "But didn't Clark love you?"

"If you mean any particular love, I've no occasion in the world to think that he did at all more nor did he any decent person about," she answered. "He was always decent and proper in the house and I never saw anything that was out of the way between him and his wife. And as for his having any particular affection for me, I never thought of such a thing. He never had his hands on me in the way that those witnesses swore. They were mistaken about all that."

Twiggs then offered an explanation of one occasion when she and Clark were seen sitting close to one another. "Where we sat on the settee there together looking up the text in the Bible that my father had heard the minister preach from, he didn't have his arm around me at all; and he never did. We sat near together just then a little while. For I was sitting there alone at first, looking for the text. And Mrs. Clark came and put her child on my knee, while she went out for a pail of water. As I held the child on one knee and the Bible on the other, Clark came and sat down near me and said he would help me and so we happened to be seen close together. My father was there. I've not the least reason to believe Clark cared for me more, nor for any other woman. And certainly nothing at all improper."

Yeomans continued his questioning. "Didn't you know anything at all about Clark as to the death of his wife?"

"Nothing in the world," she replied. "Clark told me himself that he believed I was innocent."

The Reverend Yeomans then asked, "When did he tell you that?"

"Friday morning before he was executed. We talked across through the windows. He called to me and I answered, what do you want? He says, "I am going now very soon." I says to him, "Now do tell the truth if you did that crime, and not die with a lie." He says, "I'll never say I am guilty. I know and believe you (Mrs. Twiggs) are innocent and I will say that as a dying man, but as for saying I'm guilty, I never will."

Continuing her recollection of the conversation with Clark on the morning he was to be hung, she asked him, "Was it Dr. Yeomans that set up with you last night? He said 'no.' It was two strangers." According to Mrs. Twiggs, Clark said, "I asked Dr. Yeomans to go with me on the scaffold and he would not consent. He is afraid I am denying the truth. But I will never say I am guilty. They are the very words he said to me."

At that point, Dr. Yeomans made this notation in his interview. He wrote, "This is incorrect. He (Clark) may have told her wrong or she may have forgotten the particular thing I declined doing. He did not ask me to go on the scaffold. He expected that of course from my having consented, at his request, to attend him while he lived. He had asked me to administer the communion to him, and I had declined indirectly, not being satisfied with his religious state. She (Mrs. Twiggs) seemed not positive that that was the exact thing he said I refused to do, but thought it was some such thing."

Continuing her conversation with Dr. Yeomans, Mary Twiggs asked, "Can you do anything for me? If it should please Goodness to let me live and not take me out of the world in this dreadful way. There is my poor old father and my children, and though I've got nothing but these good hands, I could make a home for them and with the blessing of Goodness I could provide for them. That makes me want to live so bad. I should be shamed indeed, if I was pardoned; for everybody would take me for guilty when I'm innocent, but still I want to live for my children and father, with all the shame so if you can do anything to save my life I know you will."

The Reverend Dr. Yeomans answered, "I don't know what can be done for you. I'll see you soon again."

Doctor Yeomans returned the following day and found Mrs. Twiggs in chains. "I suppose you think there was no need of putting that chain on you in this room. If you should break through this wall, you couldn't get over the wall of the yard."

"I shan't try any more to get out," she remarked. Her face brightened with a calm smile as she continued her explanation. "I doubt you'll not believe me, but Saturday night I went on my knees by the bedside to ask the Heavenly Father if he would help me to get out. And then I pulled the nail out that was sticking in the wall to hang clothes on and I went to work. I was so sick I could hardly stand on my feet. I worked as long as I could bear it, and then went and stood by the window. (I) saw the shadow of the gallows on the wall by the moonlight and it made me feel so bad that I went back to work again and got several stones loose in the wall before morning. Sunday night I got so far that I could see through the wall. But I didn't succeed, and now I'll not try anymore. If I can't be let out now in a regular way, and if it is the will of Heaven that I should die on the scaffold, I will say no more."

She then asked Yeomans, "But sir, won't the people that is the means of taking my life unjustly, have to answer?"

"Everyone that does wrong must answer to God. There is no getting away from Him," answered Yeomans.

"I think it will be all the same to Him, when I don't deserve it, if I die on the gallows as if I died another way. Think it will not, sir?" she asked.

"All the same. He'll think none the worse of you for that if you've not done the deed you die for," he answered.

Mrs. Twiggs then asked another question. "And don't you think sir that he'll take away all the shame for me with other people, so that them that's injured me will be ashamed nor I shall, and He'll give me more of his goodness nor He would if they hadn't been so cruel to me?"

"Certainly he will," he told Mrs. Twiggs. "But what if you are saying what isn't true now?"

She replied, "He knows doesn't He, sir? So it is, a poor helpless woman like me, put in here can't be believed a word she says, as if I was outta here and with them that knows me. So I must bear that, mustn't I, sir?"

The minister replied, "I want to believe you, and I'm trying to see good reason if I can in all that you are saying that you are telling me the truth."

"I know you do sir and I am so thankful that you come to see me, and I can talk to you better now to anybody else. And I will tell you everything I know about all these things just as if I was standing before the Heavenly Father. For what should I tell a lie to Him for?" she asked. "As I am going to die after so little, what should I make me better by telling you a word that isn't true?"

Yeomans answered, "You may think you couldn't be pardoned if you were really guilty. But you are very wrong if you think you can make your prospects any better by denying the truth. You see how it was with Clark. He gained nothing by denying and if he did lie, think how it must be with him now. God will do better for those who tell all the truth, than for those who deny it. And you know he has you in his hands now, just as much as he will when you are dead. He has the hearts of all the people in his hands who are dealing with you."

"Just so, sir," she agreed. "And how can I tell you what is not true? Oh, I do wish while you are talking to me you could see my heart as He does! Will you please sir to have confidence in me now, and then remember when we come there?" (Apparently referring to her trip on the gallows.)

"Who do you think were the means of bringing you here unjustly?" Yeomans asked.

"The people that thought I gave poison to Mrs. Clark when I was taking care of her, and that swore I bought poison at the store when I never did, and that swore such false things about seeing Clark and me together!" she replied.

"Did you believe all Clark said on the scaffold?" asked Yeomans.

"He said a great deal as I didn't know anything about. But all he said about Mr. McMullen is true, every word. And he didn't tell it all, for I know some things about it that he didn't know. He said true about my husband's being took sick by the table and going out to throw up when he'd just come from McMullen's house."

"Ah, how was that?" he asked.

"Didn't Clark nor anybody tell you about the dog?"

"No, how was it?"

"I'd like to tell ye the whole story, but maybe you haven't time, or wouldn't care to hear it."

"Well" he asked, "What about the dog?"

Mrs. Twiggs continued her story,

> We had a dog that McLaughlin gave us, a good-natured harmless creature, and he was lying on the steps. He barked at McMullen as he was going by and he (McMullen) threw a stone or bit of brick at the dog and it hit the door. David Twiggs, my husband, went to the door and said 'What did ye do that for? The dog hurts nobody!' McMullen spoke angry and David shut the door. It was Saturday evening. McMullen threw another stone against the door after a little while and David opened the door and told him to quit."

> Then, Daniel McMullen said "I'll stone you if you say a word!" David said, "Dan, I'll say no more to you now, but talk about in a day or two." Monday they met, and Dan said "Well, have you been good long enough now to talk to me again?" David said "Oh, let's not quarrel Dan, we've been good neighbors the time past. Let's be good neighbors

again." And then McMullen came up to strike him. And David got out of his way and came home. Dan followed him a piece, and says, "I've to fight with you yet. I will have your life or you'll have mine before the fourth of July!"

David was afraid of Dan and wanted to move to Philadelphia to get out of his way. But I said, "Oh no, it can all be made up, I hope." (On) Easter Sunday then McMullen sent his daughter to ask my husband to come to his house and he wouldn't go. After a little, Dan came himself and Twiggs and Clark both went with him to his house. At dinner time I sent for them and they came, my father had come home from Mr. Collins church. And at the table just after he sat down Twiggs took very bad and went out and threw up. Clark said they had drunk punch at McMullen's. He said that all along. He said it on the scaffold. Twiggs was very bad. I went out to him. He says to me, "I feel so awful, as if you was rolling your hand over in my stomach." Some days after, McMullen came and David was still sick in bed, and McMullen said to him, "Nothing ails you but ague and here is some medicine that cures ague without fail." David was a mind to take it. I said wait 'till the doctor comes, he has ague medicine. But he took it. He got no better, but was worse till he died."

"Did you ever see Clark taken ill anytime while his wife was sick?" Dr. Yeomans asked.

"Yes," replied Mrs. Twiggs. "He was lying on the back side of the bed which his wife was on, and his wife called me. "Come here quick," says she, "William is dead!" I went and took him by the shoulder and pulled him over the side and got him in a chair. He was bleeding fast at the nose.

Mrs. Hughes was in the other room, and came in to help, and pinched the nose to stop the blood, and I told her she was stopping his breath. She let go, and we got him out in the other room and laid him on the settee and after a little he came to. He had been fainty like, and didn't know nothing."

"You know that is a part of Clark's story. Is it true?" Yeomans queried.

"That is all true," Mrs. Twiggs insisted. "I tell you more (than) Clark knew; for he didn't know nothing a long while. Mrs. Hughes will remember all about it."

Dr. Yeomans added a note on the paper on which he was writing Mrs. Twiggs' remarks.

He said, "I have called on Mrs. Hughes since, and she gave substantially the same account. Mrs. Hughes is a Catholic," he continued, "Clark and (his) wife when they came to town lived first, in the second story of the Hughes house. Mrs. Hughes said Clark always treated his wife well while they were there, and never was harsh to her, though he had occasion. She (Clark's wife) would "accidently take a drink," according to Mrs. Hughes and was sometimes in bed at supper time and when Clark came to his supper and found none, he would go quietly back to work without it. Mrs. Hughes told me further, what I will here mention, that Clark talked with her privately one day, and said he was dreadfully tried with that woman, (his wife) and would leave her if it were not for his boy, (their only child at the time). He said, that when he was married to her he did not know it, the friends had made him drink till he became drunk, and when he came to himself next morning, they told him he was married to her."

Dr. Yeomans continued in his notation, "Mrs. Hughes said further that after they moved out of their house into another a few doors below, Clark became abusive to her, and she (Mrs. Clark) often came to her with her troubles. None of these things were in evidence in court. The counsel have told me they never heard of these before."

Reverend Doctor Yeomans visited Mrs. Twiggs on October 5 and found the woman busily involved in a sewing project. "I see you are making a shirt," Dr. Yeomans remarked as he entered the prison cell.

"Yes, I am and it is the saddest thing I ever did!" Mrs. Twiggs answered. "It seems like the last thing I shall ever do for the little creature. My dear little boy, oh my dear little boy. He's seven years old and here's his mother that he's not to see again in this world, and that's to be put to death in such a way for a thing that she never did, nor knew anything about. Oh, how hard it is!" (Weeping bitterly and in silence.)

(After a long pause) "I suppose there is no chance for me to be pardoned for this, so that I could be tried on the indictment for the death of my husband, is there sir?"

"Do you think you would be acquitted?"

"Oh yes," Mrs. Twiggs asserted. "Many think I caused his death but there couldn't be no proof at all, and it would give me a chance to bring in things that couldn't come in at all in the other trial, which would show that I am not guilty of either the one nor the other."

Dr. Yeomans made note that he then picked up on a prior conversation with Mrs. Twiggs and a subsequent conversation he had with Mrs. Hughes involving the drinking habits of Clark's wife.

He asked Mrs. Twiggs, "Did you ever know that Mrs. Clark drank liquor?"

"I have never told she did, for I would not talk against my neighbors. But as you ask me, I'll tell you I never saw her worse for liquor with my own eyes but once, and that was when I was in her house helping her sew. She brought out liquor and drank herself and offered me. I didn't drink. She soon got bad and didn't know what she was doing. It was Saturday afternoon. I heard she was in liquor again Sunday morning, but didn't see her. That's all I know of my own knowledge about her drinking."

Yeomans asked, "Was it common talk that she was a drinking woman?" Mrs. Twiggs replied she didn't know if it was.

Dr. Yeomans returned to the woman's prison cell the following day. "I see you have a dress partly made here."

"Yes, it's for my daughter 10 years old, an old dress of mine that I'm making into one for her."

"Then you know how to do such work?" he asked. "Yes, I can do almost any sort of work that comes across me. But my poor children, what will they do?" she lamented.

Yeomans said, "It is hard, indeed, for you, and for them, but you must commit them to Him who pities and takes care of the orphan children."

"Yes, I know the Heavenly Father is kind to them and will provide. But," she added sorrowfully, "to have them shamed always to remember and to be told that their mother died such a death as this and all that, when I don't deserve it, not at all, no more nor an infant child would."

Dr. Yeomans answered, "You must pray then, and plead your innocence to your Heavenly Father, and He is the defender of the innocent and what you say to him will be true."

"Yes, I do pray, and I have told you not one word but truth. When I'm dead, ask them that know about all I said, and you will find not a word of mine untrue. It is solemn for one under oath to lie, but would it not be solemner for me as I'm just going to die? Oh, if you would have confidence in me."

Mrs. Twiggs then pleaded with Dr. Yeomans, "Can't you come again until Monday? Four or five days. How can I go so long and not see you. But do come sooner if you can."

No other written record of conversations between Mrs. Twiggs and the Reverend Doctor Yeomans was found, other than the letter he wrote to the Governor of Pennsylvania to please for a pardon for Mrs. Twiggs.

The Reverend Dr. Yeomans final visit with Mary Twiggs was on October 6, 1858. She would be hanged on October 22. Dr. Yeomans did not accompany her to the gallows.

CHAPTER 12

As the date of Mary Twiggs' execution drew nearer, there was a concerted effort in the community to seek a pardon for her from Pennsylvania's Governor, William F. Packer.

Shortly after Mrs. Twiggs' conviction, E. H. Baldy, her attorney, sent a letter on June 1, to the Governor, asking him to talk with the presiding Judge, Alexander Jordan, before sentencing the woman to death.

The Judge did discuss the case with the governor, as referenced in a letter he sent to him on October 9, less than two weeks before the execution date. He strongly felt evidence during her trial did not warrant the guilty verdict.

His Excellency William F Packer
Governor of the Commonwealth of Pennsylvania

Dear Sir,

I had two brief conversations with you in reference to Mary Twiggs now in Montour County jail under sentence of death. On both occasions I think I stated, that had I been on the jury, I would have hesitated to convict her on the testimony produced against her. Clark, as your Excellency knows, has been executed, protesting his innocence to the last, and declaring his belief in the innocence of Mrs. Twiggs.

The accompanying papers were sent to you from Danville with a request I would forward them to Your Excellency. The petitions are numerously signed. Among the signatures will be found those of some of the witnesses, particularly the medical witnesses. There in is also a letter from Dr. Yeomans, a Presbyterian clergyman of undoubted piety and acknowledged talent, also frequent conversations he has had with the unfortunate woman.

There is to me something so abhorrent in the idea of executing a woman that I would be glad she could be pardoned. It is my duty, a duty I aver to you to state, that there is no doubt but Mrs. Clark and Mr. Twiggs were poisoned, and yet the evidence did not in my judgment establish her guilt so satisfactorily as to preclude the idea of her innocence.

You will have all the evidence before you, and the charge of the Court. I know you will examine all the documents with the care the case demands, and I am sure the conclusion to which you may arrive, and be sure as your sense of duty dictates.

The indictment for the murder of her husband is still pending against her. A pardon in the case in which she was tried and convicted would still leave her liable for trial in the other, if that was also embraced.

This case has given me great pain. I believe I did my duty and nothing more. Certainly I gave them both the benefit of the principle of the law I could.

With Great respect
Your Servant,
A. Jordan

The woman's brother, Samuel McClintock, was the first to begin circulating petitions. Among the petitions and letters seeking a pardon for Mrs. Twiggs was one from the Montour Iron Works, with signatures from many of the workmen, and the owners themselves, JP and John Grove.

Montour Ironworks Danville
18 October 1858
His Excellency William F Packer
Governor State of Pennsylvania

Dear Sir,

You are aware that Mrs. Twiggs is now in the jail of this county and to be executed for the murder of Mrs. Clark, on Friday next, and as we are among those who do not believe that the evidence produced against her, at her trial, was sufficient to warrant her conviction, we feel constrained to write this letter to you, and ask you to pardon her.

Both David Twiggs, the husband of this unfortunate woman, and William J. Clark, who was executed here last month, were employed by us in attendance of hours, living together in one of the houses of this company. We have no personal interest in this woman, and do not know her personally, but the cause of humanity and the fear of shedding innocent blood prompts us to address this letter to you in her behalf.

There was never any proof produced against her that she ever had or bought any poison--only that she was nursing Mrs. Clark, and gave her some warm drinks during her sickness, and that she and Clark seem to be very intimate, which, it is said consisted in Clark throwing his arm around her. The parties occupied the same house to save the expense of the sick— this is common among those classes having small families, and this circumstance caused the public to take it for granted that if Clark is guilty, Mrs. Twiggs must of course also be guilty, and this outside pressure and prejudice operated upon the jury unconsciously, and resulted in her conviction.

There is no proof here that this woman bought any poison or that she had any in her possession— and in nursing and giving warm drinks to a sick neighbor, who was living with her in the same house, there is certainly nothing criminal in that, as others of her neighbors done the same thing, and particularly her husband (Clark), who had bought poison and was her general nurse, and yet strange to say upon this evidence, resting upon the alleged intimacy with Clark, which is the sum and substance of the evidence produced against her, is based for her condemnation.

To think there is nothing criminal in the alleged intimacy with Clark, because there was nothing proven except that Clark was seen with his arm around her — once on a Sunday in the presence of her father, reading the Bible verse about. To form this belief from our knowledge and our life of experience among, and with these classes of people (both parties being Irish), as it is universally known that many of them are raised together in small hovels, in their country, where several families lived together in the smallest cabins, which begets a freedom of manners, without being criminal or anything thought of among themselves, to which people unused to these classes take exceptions; and you can therefore not infer that from such a trifling circumstance of intimacy, a criminal connection existed which led to a conspiracy to murder the wife of Clark by Mrs. Twiggs. There is many a woman living at these works against whom might have been proved as much as there was against this unfortunate woman— but she had the misfortune to live in the same house with a bad neighbor, who has already suffered the extreme penalty of the law, which seems to be the extent of her crime and guilt, and whose guilt has raised the unjust cry of crucify — crucify—against her.

It is an old maxim that says "It were better that 99 guilty ones should escape then that one innocent one should suffer"— and to say the worst against her, there are certainly grave doubts existing— and no proof as to her guilt, and the mercy of the laws shows that shield around the unfortunate, but whereof the jury who found her guilty did not, in consequence of the excitement of Clark's guilt, give her the benefit; and we do therefore in the most solemn manner, beseech you in the name of the all merciful God to exercise that power— the (?) resort, which the laws of the land have reposed in you to pardon those whom circumstances may place in the awful condition of this most unfortunate woman, who is the daughter of a heart-broken and aged father, and who is the mother of a poor helpless and heartbroken little daughter, who is very much attached to her poor mother, and who could not for a long time be kept out of the jail from her.

Governor will you not forgive as we all expect to be forgiven? Will you not pardon her whom the evidence does not prove guilty? Will you not give her the benefit of the certain doubts as to her guilt which hang upon the whole of this circumstantial evidence?

We in conclusion pray and beg of you to give this matter your most serious consideration; and if you have already decided against her, we again pray and beg of you to reconsider— to reconsider your decision!

In the name of humanity do not permit the hanging of a poor friendless woman and a poor mother who may be innocent.

Please telegraph to Edward H. Baldy Esq. of this place.

Very respectfully yours,
JP and J Grove

Also seeking a pardon for Twiggs was Presbyterian minister, the Rev. Dr. J. W. Yeomans, who wrote to Governor Packer on October 7.

May it please your Excellency,

I request the favor of your Excellency's attention to the following statement in behalf of Mary Twiggs, now in the jail of Montour County, under sentence of death as accomplice to William J. Clark in the murder of his wife by poison.

Clark was executed on the 24th of September. According to the sentence of the court, and the warrant of your Excellency, and without confessing his guilt. He declared, indeed, on the scaffold, and in the strongest terms as he had frequently done before in private, that he believed her to be entirely innocent. But that declaration, with the denial of his own guilt, is entitled to no weight when taken, as it is by many, with what was the deficiency of the evidence on which she was convicted.

I did not witness the trial of Clark. I was present during that of the woman and received the most decided impression that she ought not to be convicted on the evidence, and (I) was surprised and grieved when I learned the verdict!

I was afterwards informed that his honor, Judge Jordan, did not think that the evidence warranted conviction. That he did not expect a verdict of guilty, and that if he had been on the jury he could not have assented to that verdict.

At the urgent request of Clark, I attended upon him, as his religious instructor, from the time of his conviction to his execution. Having some previous knowledge of him I was pre-possessed in his favor. But after a few visits, without the least admission of any incriminating fact on his part, and irrespective of his judicial conviction, I became decided in my judgment that he was guilty, and felt myself fully warranted to deal with him accordingly.

I was amazed at his obduracy. While his conversation with me, though mild and courteous to the last, and attended by fervid professions of religious sincerity, was yet characteristic throughout of a wary and sagacious mind and failed entirely to shake my assurance of his guilt.

When, towards the last, he seemed most like being somewhat moved by the near approach of death, apparently studied his precise and nearly uniform language of denial, suggested that he might be acting under the influence of his legal counsel, and after his execution, I was informed that he considered himself as doing so.

His most frequent form of expression was, "I will never say I'm guilty." This, in connection with an oblique and artful question of his to me respecting the religious obligation and value of a confession before the world, by a really guilty man, seemed to involve indirect concession; though in his dying speech, written weeks before, and in substance published in July last, he persisted in the boldest assertions of his innocence, and of statements implicating others. This indirect concession, seemed to give more value to his assertion of the woman's innocence, then it could otherwise claim.

From the printed notes of evidence in the charge of the court, which are forwarded here within, in compliance with the suggestion of his honor Judge Jordan, your Excellency will readily perceive the grounds for the impression that the conviction was not warranted by the testimony; that the proof of her having purchased poison as alleged was deficient; that facts alleged as proving improper intimacy between Clark and this woman were imperfectly attested, and if fully proven, could everyone be reasonably explained on the supposition of her innocence.

I have attended on the woman at her request since her conviction, and I find her case in almost all respects the opposite to that of Clark. She is a person of a weak mind, and little knowledge except of the most ordinary matters pertaining to a low sphere of life, with such religious culture as prevails amongst the humblest laboring class of Protestants in Ireland; with an artless simple energy such as she exhibited in a recent attempt to escape. As an indication of her mental character and state of mind, I send here with some notes of my conversations with her since the execution of Clark.

From the great intellectual disparity between the two, anyone not unfavorably predisposed, would readily presume that Clark, with his full opportunity, might, even granting the improper intimacy, have chosen to proceed in his deed of murder without her knowledge.

This communication in the accompanying papers are transmitted through the hands of His Honor Judge Jordan, who has kindly offered to communicate to your Excellency such papers as may be sent to him for that purpose; together with his own impressions of the case.

Among the papers your Excellency will observe, a petition numerously signed by citizens of Danville and other parts of the county; drawn and signed shortly after the conviction, while the public excitement was at its height against the prisoners. The paper was circulated under great disadvantage by her (Mrs. Twiggs) brother and it is my belief that now such a paper in suitable hands would be signed much more extensively.

But for this there is not time. I would add that my anxiety in behalf of this woman is entirely that of a disinterested person, who from a clear knowledge of the case is persuaded that under all the circumstances we should not be justified in taking her life.

I do therefore, as in duty bound, most earnestly, command to the favorable consideration of your Excellency the case of this prisoner as here with presented and humbly trust that besides its appeal to the natural feelings of humanity, in behalf of one who, if guilty, may be so reasonably presumed to have been the victim and tool of a stronger mind.

Your Excellency may also discern the appeal to justice, in a case in which the judicial testimony leaves so many grounds for the presumption of innocence.

The whole is respectfully submitted in the humble hope that your Excellency will regard the case as having some peculiar and very urgent claims to the exercise of executive clemency. With this earnest and anxious hope, I remain,

Honored and Dear Sir, Your Excellency's Humble Servant
JW Yeomans
Danville October 7, 1858 (Over)

The time for the woman's execution is the 22nd installment. I feel exceedingly anxious on account of short time. Your Excellency will observe enclosed among the signatures to the petition, the names of Dr. William Magill and Dr. R. S. Simington, both of whom were witnesses on the trial in the latter the attending physician in both the cases of Mrs. Clark and David Twiggs.

If any further information should be needed or desired in the case, and I could receive reasonable notice, saved by middle of next week, my impressions in behalf of the unfortunate woman have become so strong, that I will cheerfully visit Harrisburg to communicate with your Excellency and commend the case to your Excellency's favorable consideration in person.

J. W.Y.

Despite the pleas for a pardon, Governor Packer refused to stop the execution of Mary Twiggs scheduled for October 22, 1858.

CHAPTER 13

At ten minutes past ten o'clock on Friday morning, October 22, 1858, Mary Twiggs, wearing the black dress given to her by the sheriff's wife, was taken from her prison cell. She linked arms with the Reverend Mr. Harden, the Sheriff, and other spiritual advisors who accompanied her as she walked to the scaffold.

Crying loudly, she climbed the steps slowly yet steadily, and on reaching the platform was seated on a chair. The Reverend Mr. Stover then read the 15th Chapter of Luke, while, overcome with emotion, the woman continued to cry.

Sheriff Edward Young directed Mrs. Twiggs to speak if she had something to say. Gaining composure, she answered loudly and firmly.

> This is a hard death, and the Savior has died for me, and I fear not death. I never seen or know anything about the poisoning of Catherine Ann Clark or my husband.

> I fear not death, I have nothing to regret, only the leaving of my orphan children. The Lord gave, and the Lord has taken away.

Reverend Harden then made a solemn prayer on her behalf, whereupon the ministers standing with her on the platform said goodbye. She thanked them for their kindness and again burst into tears after they shook hands and left the platform.

The Sheriff then pulled the black cap over Mary Twiggs' face, pinioned her arms, and adjusted the rope around her neck. As the final preparations were being handled she cried aloud repeating several times: *"I die innocent, I am not guilty."*

Sheriff Young then left the platform, and standing upon the steps, with the lever in his hand, he asked, "Mary Twiggs, are you still alive?" She answered, "Yes sir, I am."

At precisely 10:30 a.m., the drop fell and her soul was ushered into eternity. After hanging for 38 minutes, she was pronounced dead by the physicians and the Sheriff's jury which had been assembled to pronounce upon the death. Her body was then lowered into a coffin.

The doors of the jail yard were then thrown open, and the large crowd, which had been standing outside all morning, eagerly pressed in to get a glimpse of her body. Just as in the Clark execution, sheriff's deputies and two military units, the "Columbia Guards" and "Montour Rifles," kept order among the spectators.

The coffin was then closed, placed upon a wagon, and taken by her brother to a farm where he lived in Little Roaring Creek where she was placed in a grave.

How would you vote?

More than 160 years have passed since the executions of Mary Twiggs and William Clark.

The facts as presented during the trials for the condemned prisoners definitively indicate their spouses died from arsenic poisoning. However, did the testimony and evidence at trial prove, beyond a shadow of doubt, that Twiggs and Clark murdered Catherine Ann Clark?

Kindly note, no one was ever charged for murdering David Twiggs.

Most of the information from each prisoner's trial was found in various newspaper accounts of 1857 and 1858. At that time, there were no court stenographers to record word-for-word testimony from the witnesses who were called before the court.

After reading the previous evidence and testimony, what would you have voted on behalf of each defendant if you had been a member of the jury during one or the other of their trials? Was there enough evidence to require guilty verdicts? Don't forget that women were not able to serve on Pennsylvania juries until 1921, so Mary Twiggs was judged by a panel of 12 men.

Do you suppose a review of the evidence using a 21st century lens would lead to guilty verdicts? Or would you have voted "not guilty" (not innocent, but "not guilty").

In reading the stories of Mary Twiggs' and William Clark's trials, it is easy to forget that the first person who died was David Twiggs. If the first trial that had been held had been for the death of Mary Twiggs' husband, would the resulting verdicts have been the same? Please recall the story of Dan McMullen and how he threw rocks at the Twiggs' dog and how David Twiggs was afraid of him. Also, David Twiggs became ill on the evening he visited the McMullen house with Clark and David Twiggs died shortly after.

When David Twiggs' body was exhumed, Dr. Simington ruled that he had died of arsenic poisoning.

Is it possible that the Easter punch at McMullens' house had been laced with arsenic?

The testimony of the clerks from the pharmacy was very incriminating at the trials for Catherine Clark's murder. If Mr. Twiggs' murder trial had been held before the rumors about Mrs. Twiggs and Mr. Clark began, would a different person have been tried for David Twiggs murder?

Would an earlier trial have "recolored" the opinions of the community about Mary Twiggs and William Clark?

Testimony in Clark's February 1858 trial for the murder of his wife opened with Doctor

Robert Simington testifying that arsenic was found in Catherine Ann Clark's stomach.

Charlotte McMullen, the wife of the neighbor who threw stones at the Twiggs' dog, testified she visited a day or two after Mrs. Clark's return from Philadelphia and Mrs. Clark appeared to be coming out of a fit. At Clark's trial, she also testified she visited Mrs. Clark during the illness and brought her oil in whiskey and tea to the home. She said other women were also present during some of her frequent visits.

Aren't you glad these ladies weren't treating you during your dying days? What else was in the whiskey and tea besides oil?

Mrs. McMullen testified she later visited the sick woman on a number of occasions and at one point told William Clark that the rumors floating around town said he had poisoned his wife.

Mrs. McMullen said he denied the accusation. You will recall that Mrs. McMullen also told the court she asked Mrs. Clark directly if she felt her husband had poisoned her, and she had said "no."

Don't you wonder how much Mrs. McMullen's observations influenced the neighbors' feelings about Clark and Twiggs having a relationship?

It seems apparent that Mary Twiggs never mentioned the incidents with the McMullens prior to her trial for murdering Mrs. Clark. Nor did William Clark.

It is also obvious that none of the attorneys had asked their clients if there was anyone who "would have a reason to dislike them."

Curtis Herrington, a clerk at *Chalfant and Hughes Drugstore* in Danville, testified he recognized Clark as the man to whom he had sold magnesia, arsenic and strychnine on separate visits to the drugstore. Might he have been mistaken in his identification? His associate, Robert McCarty, wilted under cross-examination in Mary Twiggs trial and his testimony was compromised.

Do not forget that there was no written record of the purchases that were supposedly made.

Witnesses Andrew J. Thompson and John Stewart, who had known Clark when he worked at the iron works in Phoenixville, both testified they visited him in jail in May following his arrest. At that time he told them he denied buying any poison from Herrington.

Thompson also told the court he had received a letter from Clark dated August 20, 1857, asking Thompson to bring exact amounts of the poisons Clark had purchased and sneak them into prison on a future visit. Thompson turned the letter over to the authorities. Montour County Sheriff Edward Young testified that the letter was in William Clark's handwriting. However, the letter is written in a primitive style and Clark's handwriting was quite skilled. Additionally, it is doubtful that the sheriff was a handwriting expert.

The big question is, "What would Clark have wanted with the exact amounts of arsenic and strychnine?" Did he want to

demonstrate the large size of the amount he was supposed to have purchased?

At Clark's trial, four witnesses testified as to Clark's alleged intimacy with Mrs. Twiggs, frequent visits between them, and excessive familiarity.

The trial testimony indicated Clark had his arm around Mrs. Twiggs shoulder on one occasion while they were reading the Bible. She said Mrs. Clark had given her the baby to hold and Mr. Clark was helping her find a passage in the Bible. Additionally, William McClintock, the father of Mary Twiggs who lived with her, testified that he never saw anything improper between the two, and that he never saw the two together past ten o'clock. McClintock also told the court that one of the witnesses who testified as to the alleged intimacy was not on good terms with his daughter.

William Stahl, a new witness, testified that he had seen Mrs. Twiggs and Clark sitting along the creek one morning at four o'clock. Stahl said Clark had his arm around her neck. Peter Foley, who was with Stahl said he was positive of their identity although he had not seen them together on other occasions.

Are you convinced there is sufficient evidence to believe Mary Twiggs and William Clark were involved in a relationship?

Dennis Emery, a co-worker of William Clark, told the court that Clark was of good character. Emery described him as industrious, peaceful and affectionate to his wife. He said David Twiggs was Clark's helper in the iron mill and they appeared to be good friends.

Thompson Foster also gave Clark a good character reference and testified he had gone with Clark to seek out Doctor Simington when Catherine Ann Clark became ill, although Simington was not in his office at the time.

No one from William Clark's place of employment offered any negative observations about him.

After Mary Twiggs' conviction, the judge at the trial and the minister who counseled her before her execution both wrote letters to the governor asking him to pardon her. Mrs. Twiggs' brother circulated petitions and the Grove Brothers wrote to the governor on her behalf.

Do these requests for pardon influence your belief about Mary Twiggs' fate?

What do you think?

Are you convinced of William Clark's guilt in the death of his wife, Catherine Ann Clark?

Are you convinced of Mary Twiggs' guilt in the death of Catherine Ann Clark?

If you had been on each of the juries, how would you have voted? Was justice served or did one or both of the convicted murderers die as innocent victims in the 1858 hangings in Montour County?

ADDENDUM

Records dating back more than 160 years are difficult to locate. It is known that Samuel McClintock took the body of his sister Mary Twiggs to a farm in Mayberry Township where he oversaw the burial of her body. He also took custody of her children.

The 1860 Census listed Samuel as forty years of age and his occupation was listed as a day laborer. His wife, whose name was also Mary, was also forty. Two children were listed on the census: John, age 14 and Ellen, age 12. Were they the children of David and Mary Twiggs, or were they the McClintock's children? The ages would suggest they were Samuel and Mary's children. Is it possible that Samuel simply didn't list Mary's children on this census? Perhaps he was protecting them or perhaps formal adoption or guardianship was not yet accomplished.

Ten years later, in 1870, the federal census showed Samuel McClintock and his wife Mary were fifty years-old and living in Philadelphia's 23rd Ward. Also listed on the census were three children identified as Margaret, age 23, John II (author notation for clarity), age 22, and Ellen, age 19. All were listed with the last name of McClintock. The ages of the children would suggest that both boys might have been named John. If that is so, it also follows that the John who was 14 in 1860, would now be 24. Perhaps he had already moved out of the house.

Sadly, Ellen McClintock Ferguson died on May 8, 1876 and was buried in Mount Moriah Cemetery three days later. At the age of 26, she may have died in childbirth. Cemetery records at Mount Moriah Cemetery list the death of four-month-old Ellen Ferguson and her burial on September 13th of that year.

In the 1880 Census, Samuel, his wife Mary and John McClintock were listed on Stile Street in Philadelphia. Samuel's occupation was listed as a stonemason and 30-year-old John II was listed as a brick mason. JOHN II, who was 30 in 1880, would, indeed, suggest that John was Mary and David Twiggs's child.

Mary McClintock, Samuel's wife, died on March 5, 1882 at the age of 65. A death announcement in the March 8 *Philadelphia*

Inquirer invited relatives and friends to attend the funeral that afternoon at the residence of her and her husband, Samuel, on Stiles Street, below Orthodox Street in the Frankford section of Philadelphia.

The 1890 U.S. Census records were reportedly damaged in a fire and no record of Samuel McClintock is available from that year. However, Pennsylvania death records show that he died May 5, 1891 at the age of 76 and was buried four days later at Cedar Hill Cemetery in Philadelphia.

Determining the whereabouts of John II McClintock after the 1880 Census could not be established without additional information.

The hanging of Mary Twiggs drew attention from newspapers around the country, including brief mentions of the events of that day. Her death also produced a number of editorials on the issue of capital punishment.

PHILADELPHIA INQUIRER
Editorial on Twiggs Death, September 23, 1858
Execution of a Woman
Yesterday, the hangman's day, was marked at Danville, in this state, by the execution of Mrs. Mary Twiggs. "… and though many strenuous efforts have been made to save Mrs. Twiggs from the gallows, Governor Packer has seen no reason to interfere with the stern course of the law. Upon the gallows yesterday, the woman protested her innocence to the latest moment of her life. Heaven only is her judge.
WISCONSIN FREE DEMOCRAT EDITORIAL
November 3, 1858
Mrs. Mary Twiggs was recently hung at Danville, Pennsylvania for the supposed murder of Mrs. Clark. The papers state public opinion was divided as to her guilt. It is bad enough to hang any person, but to hang a woman whose offense is not so clear, but that public opinion is divided with reference to her guilt, is an act of reckless barbarism, sufficient to disgrace any people.

TRUE AMERICAN (STEUBENVILLE, OHIO)
November 10, 1858

After recapping the circumstances surrounding the case, the newspaper printed this Opinion:

Thus has the law of blood for blood had another victim. A mother supposed to be guilty of a crime has been taken from her family, and some dozen strong and able-bodied men, assisted by the military of the state of Pennsylvania, either direction and authority of her laws, after having become weak enemies emaciated by long confinement in prison, she is taken out, the cord tied around her neck and deliberately strangled to death. What for? They supposed she had poisoned a woman, on the strength of which supposition they, in turn, choked her to death.

CARLISLE WEEKLY HERALD, CARLISLE, PENNSYLVANIA
November 21, 1858
EXECUTION OF A WOMAN
We have never been the advocate of the abolishment of the death penalty, yet there is something so revolting in the public execution of a woman on the gallows, that we would be reconciled to a law that would discriminate in capital cases between the sexes. Who can read the account given, of the night before the execution of Mrs. Twiggs at Danville, without feeling sympathy for the wretched mother, nestling her hapless children on her bosom with maternal solicitude, yet conscious that the morning sun would see her hanging between heaven and earth, a victim of the law of "life for life," while the children then sleeping in her arms, would be abandoned to the pitiless scorn of the world?
Look on the picture!

ALSO …

A retelling of the Twiggs and Clark Murder cases have found their way into newspaper accounts over the years. In May of 1903, the *Danville Morning News* published a story that two men in Mayberry Township, Montour County, stumbled on the grave of Mary Twiggs.

V.A. Lotier, and Oscar Kase discovered the site in a remote area of the township. According to the newspaper article, the woman's grave was in an out-of-the-way corner of the township marked by a head and footstone and enclosed by a heavy stone wall. It was generally given a wide birth and visited only now and then because of curiosity.

When Lotier and Kase found the gravesite, the solid stone walls in the head and foot stones were overthrown, while where the grave was, there was a cavity of considerable depth. The newspaper account theorized "The general appearances such as to indicate that at some time the spot might have been visited by ghouls, who exhumed and carried off the bones. Whether or not such an event ever occurred is in this day not a matter of sufficient importance to merit an investigation."

AND …

In February 1917, some 60 years after the hangings of Mary Twiggs and William Clark, a stranger came to town with an unusual request related to the gallows that was used to hang the pair. James Fleming, Jr, a traveling salesman from Philadelphia, finding himself in the proximity of the courthouse in Danville, surprised Horace C. Blue, the clerk of the County commissioners' office, by asking Blue on the whereabouts of the gallows. Somewhat taken aback by the inquiry, the clerk said the gallows was burned in the fire which destroyed the jail some years following the executions.

Fleming explained that his mother-in-law, Mrs. John U. Smith of Philadelphia was a native of Danville: that her maiden name was Mary Diehl and that her father Charles Diehl constructed the model for the gallows. Apparently, Mrs. Smith had frequently talked about her father's role in the case and had received a promise from Fleming that should he ever find himself in Danville, he would visit the prison and view the scaffold.

Charcoal Sketch of the "Big Mill" by Larry E. Mordan

Photo Credit: Helen "Sis" Hause

William Clark was among a unique group of workmen known as puddlers,
such as those in this circa 1890's photo from the Montour Iron Works.
Montour County historian Helen "Sis" Hause shared a description of the puddlers
life in a newspaper article. It was written by James J. Davis, U.S. Labor Secretary
under President Warren Harding. Davis ws a master pubddler in earlier life.

"In the mill there is a constant din by day and night. Patches of white heat glare
from the open furnance doors like the teeth of some great dark dingy devil
grinning across the smoky vapors of the pit. Half naked soot smeared fellows
fight the furnance hearths with hooks, rabbles and paddles. "....Flaming balls of
wooly iron are pulled from the oven door, flung onto a two wheeled serving cart
and rushed sputtering and flamboyant to the hungry mouth of the squeezer."

The "puddled" liquid which came from crude pig iron was sent to the rollers
within the iron mills, to be made into rails or other products.

Rich veins of iron ore were mined from the hills of Montour County and sent to
the local mills for processing.

Photo Credit: William W. Wilt III

Built between 1817-1818 when Danville
was still part of Columbia County.
It served as Montour County Jail
until torn down in 1892.
William Clark and Mary Twiggs were hanged in the walled
prison yard in 1858.

DRUGS & MEDICINES.

THE subscribers would respectfully inform the citizens of Danville and vicinity that they have

REMOVED TO THEIR NEW BRICK BUILDING

Four doors from their old stand and one door South of Comly & Groves' Store, North Danville,

Where they have opened a fresh supply of

Drugs, Chemicals, Dye-Stuffs, Paints, Oils, Varnishes, Hair Oil, Perfumery, &c , &c.,

Which they will WARRANT to be of the first quality.

They have also obtained the agencies of a the most popular

PATENT MEDICINES.

All of which may be relied on as they have been selected with the utmost care.

CHALFANT & HUGHES.

Danville, Dec. 5, 1855.—tf

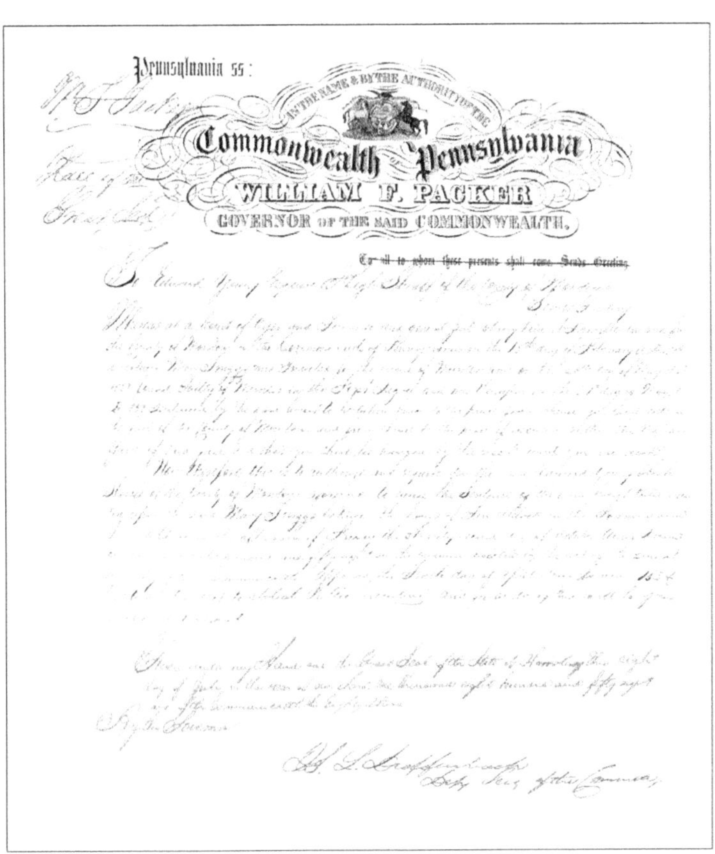

Mary Twiggs Death Warrant

PENNSYLVANIA PLACE OF THE GREAT SEAL

IN THE NAME AND BY THE AUTHORITY OF THE COMMONWEALTH OF

PENNSYLVANIA

WILLIAM F. PACKER

GOVERNOR OF THE SAID COMMONWEALTH

To Edward Young Esquire High Sheriff of the County of Montour

Whereas at a Court of Oyer and Terminer and General Jail delivery held at Danville in and for the County of Montour in the Commonwealth of Pennsylvania on the 15th day of February A.D. 1858 a certain Mary Twiggs was Indicted for the Crime of Murder. and on the 20th day of May 1858 A.D. found guilty of murder in the first degree and there upon the 21st day of May A.D. 1858 sentenced by the said court to be taken hence to the place where whence you came within the jail of the County of Montour. and from thence to the place of execution within the walls or yard of the said jail and that there you be hanged by the neck until you are dead.

Now therefore this is to authorize and request that the said Edward Young High Sheriff of the County of Montour aforesaid to cause the sentence of the said Court to be executed upon the said Mary Twiggs between the hours of ten o'clock in the forenoon and three o'clock in the afternoon on Friday the Twenty Second day of October Anno Domini One Thousand and Eight Hundred and Fifty Eight in the manner directed by the General Assembly of this Commonwealth approved the Tenth day of April Anno Domini 1834 entitled an Act to abolish public executing and for so doing this shall be your sufficient warrant.

Given under my hand and the Great Seal of the State at Harrisburg this Eighth day of July in the year of our Lord One Thousand Eight Hundred and Fifty Eight and of the Commonwealth the Eighty-third.

By the Governor

H.L. Dieffenbach   Deputy Secretary of the Commonwealth

84

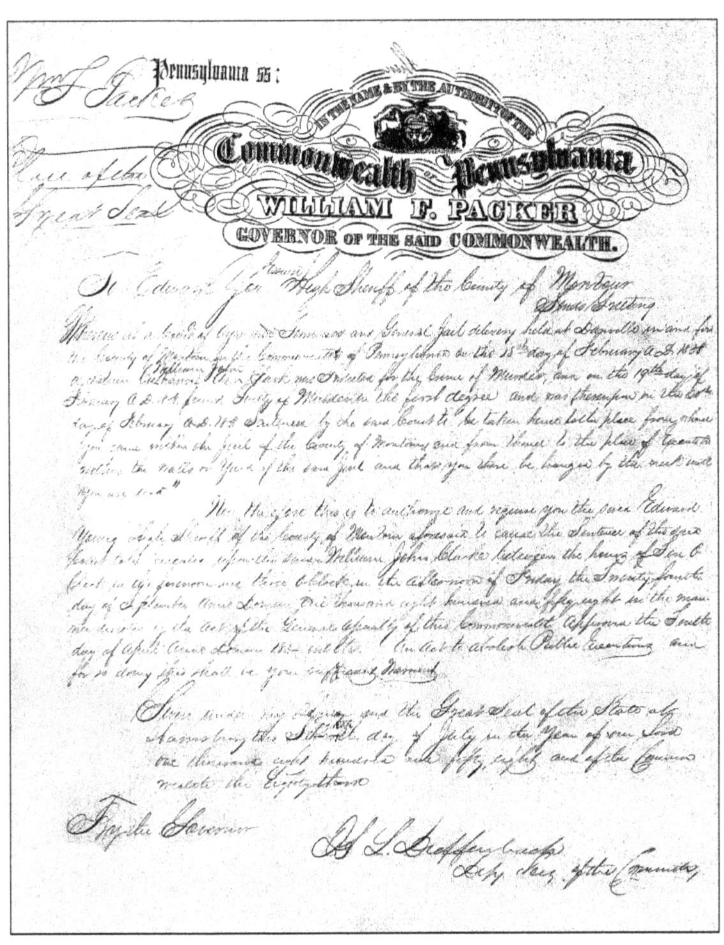

Death Warrant of William John Clark
Signed by Governor William F. Packer

PENNSYLVANIA PLACE OF THE GREAT SEAL

IN THE NAME AND BY THE AUTHORITY OF THE COMMONWEALTH OF

PENNSYLVANIA

WILLIAM F. PACKER

GOVERNOR OF THE SAID COMMONWEALTH

To Edward Young Esquire High Sheriff of the County of Montour

Whereas at a Court of Oyer and Terminer and General Jail delivery held at Danville in and forthe County of Montour in the Commonwealth of Pennsylvania on the 15th day of February A.D.1858 a certain William John Clark was Indicted for the Crime of Murder, and on the 19th day of February 1858 A.D. found guilty of murder in the first degree and there upon the 20th day of February A.D. 1858 sentenced by the said court to be taken hence to the place where whence you came within the jail of the County of Montour, and from thence to the place of execution within the walls or yard of the said jail and that there you be hanged by the neck until you are dead.

Now therefore this is to authorize and request that the said Edward Young High Sheriff of the County of Montour aforesaid to cause the sentence of the said Court to be executed upon the said William John Clark between the hours of ten o'clock in the forenoon and three o'clock in the afternoon on Friday the Twenty Fourth day of September Anno Domini One Thousand and Eight Hundred and Fifty Eight in the manner directed by the General Assembly of this Commonwealth approved the Tenth day of April Anno Domini 1834 entitled an Act to abolish public executing and for so doing this shall be your sufficient warrant.

Given under my hand and the Great Seal of the State at Harrisburg this Eighth day of July in the year of our Lord One Thousand Eight Hundred and Fifty Eight and of the Commonwealth the Eighty-third.

By the Governor

 H.L. Dieffenbach   Deputy Secretary of the Commonwealth

Montour Iron Works
Danville 18 Oct. 1858.

His Ex. Wm F Packer
Gov. State of Penna   Dear Sir

You are aware that Mrs. Twiggs
is now in the jail of this County, and to be
executed for the murder of Mrs. Clark, on
Friday next and as we are among those who
do not believe that the evidence produced against
her, on her trial, was sufficient to warrant her
conviction we feel constrained to write this
letter to you, and ask you to pardon her.

Both David Twiggs, the husband of this unfortunate woman and Wm F. Clark, who was
executed here last month, were employed by us
and tenants of ours living together in one of
the houses of this Company. We have no personal
interest in this woman, and do not know her
personally, but the cause of humanity and the

fear of shedding innocent blood prompts us to
address this letter to you in her behalf.

There never was any proof produced against
her that she ever had or bought any poison only
that she was nursing Mrs. Clark and gave her some
warm drinks during her sickness and that she and
Clark seemed to be very intimate which it is said
Consisted in Clark throwing his arm around her
The parties occupied the same house to save the ex
pense of the rent this is common among these Classes
having small families and this circumstance caused the
Publick to take it for granted that if Clark is guilty
Mrs. Twiggs must of Course also be guilty and this
out side pressure and prejudice operated upon the
jury unconsciously, and resulted in her Conviction

There is no proof then that this woman bought
any poison or that she had any in her possession.
and in nursing and giving warm drinks to a sick
neighbor who was living with her in the same house
there is certainly nothing Criminal in that as Hiss of
her neigbors does the same thing, and particularly her
husband Clark who had bought poison and was
her general Nurse and yet strange to say upon this

evidence resting upon the alledged intimacy with Clark which is the sum and substance of the evidence produced against her is based her Condemnation

We think there is nothing criminal in the alledged intimacy with Clark because there was nothing proven except that Clark was seen with his arm around her once on a Sunday in the presence of her Father reading the Bible verse about to form this belief from our knowledge and a life of experience among & with these Classes of People both parties being Irish) as it is universally known that many of them are raised together in small hovels in their Country where several families live together in the smallest Cabins which begets a freedom of manners without being criminal or any thing thought of among themselves to which People unused to these Classes take ex ceptions and we can therefore act infer that from such a trifling circumstance of intimacy a Criminal Connection existed which led to a Conspiricy to murder the Wife of Clark by Mrs. Twiggs

There is many a woman living at these Works against whom might have been proved as much as there was against this unfortunate woman but she had the misfortune to live in the same house with a bad neighbor who has already suffered the extreme penalty of the law which seems to be the extent of her crime and guilt and whose guilt has raised the unjust cry of Crucify Crucify against her. It is an old maxim that says it were better that ninety nine guilty ones should escape than that one innocent one should suffer and to say the worst against her there is certainly grave doubts existing — and no proof as to her guilt and the mercy of the law throws that shield around the unfortunate but whereof the jury who found her guilty did not in consequence of the excitement of Clark's guilt give her the benefit and we do therefore in the most solemn manner beseech you in the name of the All merciful God to exercise that power — the dernier resort which the laws of the land have reposed in you to pardon those whom circum- stances may place in the awful condition of this most unfortunate woman who is the daughter of a heart broken and aged Father and who is the Mother of a poor helpless and heart-broken little daughter

who is indeed very much attached to her poor [5]
Mother and who could not for a long time be
kept out of jail from her. —

Gov. will you not forgive as we all expect
to be forgiven? — Will you not pardon her whom
the evidence does not prove guilty? — Will you not
give her the benifit of the Certain doubts as to
her guilt which hang upon the whole this circumstantial evidence? To believe and have an abiding
faith that you will do so — and at once, as there
is now no time to be lost.

To in conclusion pray and beg of you to give
this matter your most serious consideration, and
if you have already decided against her we again
pray and beg of you to reconsider — to reconsider
your decision. In the name of humanity do not permit
the hanging of a poor friendless woman and a poor
Mother who may be innocent. —

Please telegraph to Edward A Bailey, Esq. of this place.

Very Respectfully Yours &c. J R P of Grove

6)

8)

my husband's being took sick at the table
& going out to throw up, when he'd just
come from M'Mullen's house."
    "Ah, how was that?
    "D'ye never hear? Didn't Clark nor any
body tell ye about the dog?
    "No, how was it?"
    "I'd like to tell ye the whole long story, but
may be you haven't time, or wouldn't can
to hear it.
    "Well, how about the dog?"
    "We had a dog, that M'Laughlin gave us,
a good natured harmless creature & he was
lying on the steps, & he barked at M'Mullen as he was going by, & he threw a stone
or bit o' brick at the dog, & shut the door.
& David Twiggs, my husband went to the
the door & said, What d'ye do that for? The
dog hurts nobody. M'Mullen spoke an-
gry & David shut the door. It was Saturday
evening. M'Mullen threw another stone
against the door after a little; & David opened
the door & told him to quit; & Daniel M'Mullen said, I'll stone you if you say a word.
David said, Dan, I'll say no more to you
now, but talk about in a day or two. Monday, they met & Dan said, Well, have ye
been good long enough now to talk to me
again David said, O, let's not quarrel,
Dan, we're good neighbors the time past
let's be good neighbors again. And Dan

Conversations between Mary Twiggs
and Rev. J. W. Yeomans in the weeks prior to her execution
(Chapter Eleven)

came up to strike him. And David got
out of his way & came home; & Dan foller
ed him a piece & says, I've to fight with
ye yet. I'll have your life or you'll have
mine before the fourth of July. David
was afraid of Dan, & wanted to move to
Philadelphia to get out of his way. But
I said, no, it can all be made up, I hope.
Easter Sunday, Dan, sent his daughter
to ask my husband to come to his house, &
he wouldn't go. After a little, Dan ~~himself~~
came himself, & Twiggs & Clark both went
with him to his house. At dinner time I
sent for them, & they came. My father had
come home from Mr Collins church. And
at the table just after he sat down, Twiggs
took very bad, & went out & threw up.
Clark said they had drunk punch
at Mr Mullen's; he's said that all along &
he said it on the scaffold. Twiggs was
very bad. I went out to him. He says to
me, I feel so awful, as if you was rolling
your hand over in my stomach. Some
days after Mr Mullen came; & David
was still sick in bed, & Mr M. said
to him "Nothing ails you but ague
& here is some medicine that cures
ague without fail." David was a mind
to take it. I said Wait till the doctor comes; he has ague medicine too
But he took it. He got no better

Sunbury, Oct 9 1858

In a letter to Governor William Packer
Judge Alex Jordan said based on the evidence presented
he would not have convicted Mary Twiggs
(Chapter 12)

Danville Oct 18 1858

His Excellency Wm T. Packer
Governor of the Commonwealth
of Pennsylvania:

I received early your
Excellency's telegram informing
me that you "could see no reason for Executive interference" in
the case of the prisoner Mary
Twiggs. Her afflicted brother cannot bear that the sentence should
be executed, without first entreating
your Excellency for clemency, & the
aged father would go with him but
for fear he could not endure the jour-
ney & for want of means. He carries
other papers, & I write this line by
him to assure your Excellency that
your official interposition in this case
would
~~will~~ afford great satisfaction to the
intelligent & influential portion of
this community.
With great respect I remain
Your Excellency's Obed't Serv't
J W Romans

95

William F. Packer
14th Governor of Pennsylvania
1858-1861

PENNSYLVANIA STATE REPORTS VOL. XXIX
Comprising Cases Adjudged in the Supreme Court of Pennsylvania
By
JOSEPH CASEY
State Reporter
VOL. V.
Containing
Cases Decided in May and October Terms, 1857
William John Clark versus The Commonwealth.

The refusal of the court to discharge a prisoner on the last day of the second term after his arrest, under the 3d section of the Habeas Corpus Act, is essentially a habeas corpus proceeding, and does not come up with the record on a writ of error taken by the prisoner after conviction and judgment.

A prisoner, under that act, can only claim his discharge on the last day of the second term after his arrest, when there has been a competent and regularly constituted court, before which he could have been indicted and tried?

The act was designed to prevent wrongful restraints of liberty growing out of the malice and procrastination of the prosecutor, but not to shield a prisoner in any case from the consequences of any delay made necessary by the law itself.

Where the array of grand jurors was quashed at two successive terms after the arrest of the prisoner, for informality in selecting and drawing them, he was not entitled to be discharged.
The statute requiring an addition to be given to jurors, is directory merely, and, to be a mark of identity, is properly written as it is commonly known in the community from which the juror is drawn.

The addition of "Mill Boss" to the name of a juror will be presumed to designate his occupation as known and understood in the neighbourhood where he resides.

The right of a president judge to exercise his functions within a county, attached by the legislature to his district subsequent to his election, cannot be questioned collaterally.

The court will judicially take notice of the legislation by which he claims to exercise his office, so far as to hold him a judge de facto, and as against all but the Commonwealth a judge dejure.

The right and powers of a judge de facto, with colour of title, can only be inquired into by quo warranto, at the suit of the Commonwealth. Burnell's Case, 7 Barr 34.

Error to the Oyer and Terminer of Montour county. This was an indictment charging William John Clark and Mary Twiggs with the murder of Catharine Ann Clark, the wife of plaintiff in error. The indictment consists of four counts:

The first count charges the defendants with the murder of Catharine Ann Clark, by mixing and mingling white arsenic with magnesia and water, the said defendants knowing the magnesia and water to have been prepared for the use of the said Catharine Ann Clark, and to be taken and swallowed by her.

The second count charges the defendants with the murder of Catharine Ann Clark, by administering to her white arsenic.

The third count charges the defendants with the murder of Catharine Ann Clark, alleging the mixing and mingling of white arsenic with magnesia and water by William John Clark, and that Mary Twiggs was present, aiding and abetting. Defendants knowing the said magnesia and water to have been prepared for the use of said Catharine Ann Clark.

The fourth count charges Mary Twiggs with having mixed and mingled the white arsenic with magnesia and water, and William John Clark with being present, aiding and abetting.

The defendants were committed on the charge in May, 1857. The first term of the court of Montour county thereafter commenced on the third Monday of September, and the second term on the third Monday of December, 1857. At both these terms the array of grand jurors was quashed, but not on motion of the defendants. On the last day of the December Term, Clark by his counsel moved to be discharged under the 3d section of the Habeas Corpus Act, passed 18th February, 1785, but the motion was overruled. This motion was again renewed when called upon to plead to the indictment at February Term, 1858, and again denied.

At February Term, 1858, the defendant Clark moved to quash the array of grand jurors, on the ground that Matthew S. Ridgway, one of the grand jurors on the venire, was returned without any addition of trade or mystery, estate or degree known in the law, but instead thereof has added after his name "Mill Boss." This motion was also overruled.

The defendant Clark thereupon interposed the following plea to the jurisdiction of the court:—

And now, February 16th, A. D. one thousand eight hundred and fifty-eight, William J. Clark, in his proper person, cometh into court here, and having heard the said indictment read, says that the said court here ought not to take cognisance of the felony in the said indictment specified; because protesting that he is not guilty of the same, nevertheless the said William John Clark says that the felony in the said indictment specified is triable in the Court of Oyer and Terminer of the county of Montour, and not elsewhere; that the court here purporting to be the Court of Oyer and Terminer of the county of Montour is not such court, competent for the trial of the said felony, because the Honourable Alexander Jordan, acting as president judge of the court here, is not now, nor ever has been, a judge of the Court of Oyer and Terminer of Montour county; he, the said Alexander Jordan, not having been elected a judge of the said court of Montour county, according to the provisions of the constitution of the Commonwealth of Pennsylvania; the county of Montour, at the time of the election of the said Alexander Jordan, if ever elected, formed no part of the judicial district over which he, the said Alexander Jordan, was elected to preside or act as a judge, but at the time of said election, the said county of Montour did belong to and form a part of the eleventh judicial district, composed of the counties of Luzerne, Wyoming, Columbia, and Montour, in which the Honourable John N. Conyngham was duly elected president judge, wherefore he prays judgment, if the said court, now here will or ought to take cognisance of the indictment aforesaid, and by the court here he may be dismissed or discharged, &c. To this plea the Commonwealth demurred, the defendant joined in the demurrer, whereupon the court sustained the demurrer, and gave judgment that the defendant answer over. A separate trial having been granted, the defendant Clark was arraigned, and to the several counts in the indictment he pleaded not guilty, and on the 16th February, 1858, a jury was called and sworn, and on the 19th of the same month returned a verdict of guilty of murder in the first degree, and on the following day sentence of death was pronounced against him by the court.

He thereupon applied for and obtained this writ of error, and assigned here that the court below erred in overruling the motion to discharge the prisoner on the 24th December, 1857; in denying the prisoner's application for discharge, when called upon to plead at February Term, 1858; in refusing to quash the array of grand jurors at February Term, 1858; and in overruling the plea to the jurisdiction.

Robert F. Clark, for the prisoner.—The preamble to the act discloses what it was intended to accomplish. Before its passage the courts exercised a discretionary power to discharge, and the object of the enactment was to convert into a right what the court might grant as a favour. That right was a discharge at the second term if not indicted and tried, the same as if he had been tried and acquitted.

The act makes its own exceptions. The array was not quashed upon his motion. All the facts came clearly and distinctly upon the record. The statute is a remedial one, and should be liberally and beneficially expounded in favour of the liberty of the citizen. The terms are plain and explicit, and appear to leave no room for construction. The argument ab inconvenienti can in such a case have no force.

Is the operation of this act restrained by judicial construction? These may be classed under three heads: 1st. When the trial is impossible by the rules of law, as in the case of Martin Rinner, 16 S. £ R. 304. 2d. When the trial is impossible by the act of God, as in the case of William Phillips, 7 Watts 366. 3d. When the delay is occasioned by the wrongful act of the defendant, as in Arnold and Others, 3 Yeates 263. Commonwealth v. Prophet, 1 Brown 135, is like the present, and there the prisoner was discharged: Commonwealth v. Chauncey, 2 Ash. 101. It is only when a statute is doubtful that an argument from inconvenience will have weight: 9 Bac. Ab. 240-255; 4 U. S. Con. Rep. 595.

2. The addition of "Mill Boss" is insensible. It is not, as the Commonwealth's counsel suppose, a wrong addition, but no addition at all.

3. The plea to the jurisdiction should have been sustained.

It puts in question the power of the legislature to alter a judicial district, after they have districted the state and the judges have been elected by the people of the several districts.

The amendment to the constitution provided " That the president judges of the several Courts of Common Pleas and of such other courts of record as are or shall be established by law, and all other judges required to be learned in the law, shall be elected by the qualified electors of the respective districts over which they are to preside or act as judges." The state is districted by the legislature and an election for judges is held. The right vested in the qualified voters of the several districts has been exercised, and the majority have chosen their judge. Where is the power of the legislature to alter the district after such election? By what authority does the legislature presume to abridge or nullify the right of any county to a voice in the election of the judge who is to preside in such county, and in whose election the constitution provides they shall have a voice? What more glaring invasion can there be of a constitutional right than this ?—the legislature removed from the bench of Montour county the judge of their choice, and supplied his place for nine years to come with a judge in whose election the qualified voters of such county had no voice. The power of the legislature to alter, implies the power to abolish a district. If after the state is districted and an election had, the legislature can abolish entire districts at pleasure, then the constitutional right of the people to elect their judge is a nullity.

Comly and Rhodes, for the Commonwealth.—The 1st and 2d errors assigned do not arise upon the record. Nothing can be added to the component parts of a record: Middleton v. Commonwealth, 2 Watts 286: and it is clear from this case and the Commonwealth v. Church, 1 Barr 105, that the opinion of the judge forms no part of the record. It is so in civil cases where the charge is not excepted to: Holden v. Cole, 1 Barr 303. Still less can the written reasons of the defendant below be so considered, or any evidence of the facts contained in them. Stripping the case then of the statements of defendant, and the opinions of the court, it nowhere appears when he was committed, or that he ever applied for a discharge or the court refused such a motion. The facts in such a case cannot be brought before this court. The defendant's only remedy was a writ of habeas corpus; but he cannot wait and take his chance of a trial. No defendant has yet been discharged under the Act of 1785 after trial and conviction.

If the facts could be brought before this court properly, the decision of the court below would doubtless be sustained.

2. The 38th section of the Act of 14th April, 1834, requires that the names and additions of persons selected as jurors shall be written on slips of paper, but there is no law designating or enumerating what shall be proper additions. By what criterion can it be determined that "Mill Boss" is not a proper addition? As science and the arts advance, new occupations arise, and they cannot be defined beforehand. But a few years ago " Telegraph Operator" would have been unintelligible—now it is well known and understood. The defendant was indicted with the addition of " Puddler," an occupation well known in iron manufacturing districts, but unknown to thousands in other localities.

So " Mill Boss" is a term perfectly well understood in Montour county, as a superintendent of hands in a rolling-mill, and so the juror was known. "Boss" is defined by Webster as a "superintendent." But whether it indicates, at the place of trial, an addition or occupation, is a question of fact which must be left to the court below, and the evidence cannot be removed.

The last error assigned, it appears to the counsel for the Commonwealth, cannot be sustained. The plea of the defendant is simply, and nothing more than, a challenge to the president judge which could not be allowed: 3 Bl. Com. 361. As a plea it would require him to sit as judge to decide his own right to the seat he occupied. It cannot be contended that he was not a judge de facto; and that being the case, his title to the office can only be determined by quo warranto in the Supreme Court. But he was a judge de jure. He was duly elected, by the qualified voters, president judge of the 8th judicial district, and that is the office which he now holds. The legislature added the county of Montour to his district, in the exercise of a power which it is absolutely necessary they should possess, and which is denied to them by no section of the constitution. The case of the Commonwealth v. McClean, 4 Yeates 399, is full to the point. C. J. Tilghman says (page 400), "when the present constitution was framed, it was well understood that the power of altering counties had always been exercised by the legislature, and that it was necessary that power should continue. It was understood, too, that certain consequences necessarily flowed from the alteration of counties. In construing the constitution, therefore, we must take care not to destroy those implied powers, without which society could not exist." All this applies as strongly to the alteration of judicial districts. In this case, it was decided that a justice of the peace, commissioned during good behaviour, who resided in the part cut off from the county, for which he was commissioned, ceased to be a justice—that the jurisdiction of a justice of the peace increased or diminished as the county increased or diminished. On the same principle Judge Conyngham's jurisdiction decreased, when Montour county was taken from his district, and Judge Jordan's was increased, when the same county was added to his, and the vested rights of no one were affected by the change.

The opinion of the court was delivered by Woodward, J.

The plaintiff in error, William John Clark, having been convicted and sentenced for murder in the first degree, in the Court of Oyer and Terminer of Montour county, removes the record into this court, and assigns four several errors, which are to be considered in order. The first and second errors may be considered together, as they both relate to the refusal of the court to discharge Clark under the provisions of the third section of the Habeas Corpus Act of 18th February, 1785, after he had been held in confinement two terms without indictment or trial.

The first motion for his discharge on this ground was made on the 24th December, 1857, which the court on the same day denied. Then again, on the 16th February, 1858, when he was arraigned, he put in a written refusal to plead on two grounds, one of which was this confinement for two terms and more without trial, although he was ready for trial at both of the terms of court which had intervened. The court again refused to discharge him, and directed a plea of not guilty to be entered for him.

These two applications for discharge were essentially habeas corpus proceedings, though not such in form. They were grounded upon the habeas corpus statute, and the power invoked was that which the court exercises under the writ of habeas corpus, and in no other manner. Viewed in this light, they were distinct and separate from the proceedings which are brought up by our writ of error. They form no part of this record, and are not necessarily or regularly brought up with it. If the judgment of the court in a habeas corpus case were reviewable here, which it is not except on another writ of habeas corpus issued out of this court, the writ of error which we allowed to the prisoner was not directed to that judgment and did not bring it up. It is perfectly manifest, therefore, that the question raised by the first two assignments of error is not regularly here, and we would be quite justifiable in declining to express any opinion upon it.

Considering, however, that the prisoner's life is at stake, and that his counsel have enabled us to form an opinion on the point by presenting all the necessary documents, and accompanying them with an able and instructive argument, we will, for their satisfaction, allude briefly to the ground on which we think the learned judge of the Oyer and Terminer was right in refusing to discharge the prisoner from confinement. The Act of 18th February, 1785, in its title and preamble, shows that it was designed to prevent "wrongful" restraints of liberty. The third section, after providing that any person committed for treason or felony, and not tried some time in the next term, session of Oyer and Terminer, general jail delivery, or other court after such commitment, shall, upon the last day of the term, sessions, or court be set at liberty upon bail, goes on to say: "and if such prisoner shall not be indicted and tried the second term, sessions, or court after his or her commitment, unless the delay happen on the application, or with the assent of the defendant, or upon trial shall be acquitted, he or she shall be discharged from imprisonment." Now, the evident construction of this section is, that the "term, session, or court" intended by the act is a legally constituted and competent term, session, or court. It meant that a prosecutor should not allow two such terms or sessions of the court, at each of which the defendant might be legally indicted or tried, to elapse without bringing on the prosecution. But to constitute a competent court, several things are necessary: the presence of the president judge and jurors, grand and petit, drawn, summoned, and impannelled according to law. Time is another legal requisite. Many president judges are required to hold Courts of Oyer and Terminer in different counties on certain prefixed days; and if the number or duration of trials in one county prevent him from trying all the cases before the law requires his presence elsewhere, the prisoners, whom it has been impossible to try, are not to take advantage of this ineffectual term to claim their release. It is only after two terms, at both of which it was possible to indict and try them according to law, that they become entitled to a discharge. The statute was made to restrain the malice and oppression of prosecutors, and to relieve wrongful imprisonment; not to embarrass the administration of the criminal law; not to relieve righteous imprisonment, and to defeat public justice. Such was the construction which this section received from this court in the case of the Commonwealth v. The Sheriff and Jailer of Allegheny County, 16 S. $t R. 304, wherein it was held that a prisoner indicted for aiding and abetting another to commit murder, and not tried at the second term, was not entitled to his discharge on habeas corpus when proceedings to outlawry against the principal had been commenced without delay, but there had not been time to finish them. The language of Judge Todd, speaking for the whole court, was very much in point: "What, then," said he, "was the third section of the act intended to provide against? I think it was intended to provide against the abuse of procrastinated trial, to provide not only against the malice of the prosecutor, and against his negligence, against all his delays with cause or without cause, against every possible act or want of action of the prosecutor; but not to shield a prisoner in any case from the consequences of any delay made necessary by the law itself."

The only authority invoked against this doctrine is an unreasoned judgment of the Common Pleas of Philadelphia, in 1810, reported in 1 Brown 135, which scarcely deserves to be mentioned. If, then, this prisoner, instead of appealing to the court as upon habeas corpus, had pleaded his new trial at the September and December Terms which elapsed after his full commitment, and thus had brought the question upon the present record, it could not have availed him. It may be well doubted whether upon demurrer such a plea would not have been set aside as wholly insufficient to bar the prosecution, but it is certain the plea would have been fully answered by a replication that no legal panel of jurors had been summoned at these terms. And if to such a replication the defendant had demurred, judgment must inevitably have gone against him, for the delay would have been attributable to the law itself. A panel of jurors, constituted according to law, was as necessary an ingredient of a competent court as the president judge himself; and delay in constituting it was as truly the law's delay as that which is caused by the necessary forms of outlawry.

It is no answer to urge that the sheriff and commissioners, who were the officers of the law, caused the delay by not drawing and summoning jurors aright. The statute which the prisoner invokes was not designed to give him this benefit of official negligence. As a member of society he was represented by those officers; and when he entered upon a course of crime, and placed himself in antagonism to society, he assumed the risk of their performing their duties so faithfully as to speed the penalty. It seems to his advantage that they did not—but to his advantage only in giving him more time for repentance—not as furnishing grounds for his discharge. The dilatoriness of the agents, who in some sense were his own agents, cannot cancel his responsibilities to society. He is not in position to take advantage of it in the manner proposed.

Nothing is lost to the defendant, therefore, by his failing to plead in bar the matter urged upon the judge as ground of discharge. Our judgment would have been against him on such a record as much as it is upon the record now before us.

The third error assigned is upon the court's overruling the motion to quash the array of grand jurors at February Term. The ground of this motion was that Mathew S. Ridgway, one of the jurors, was not sufficiently indicated by his addition or occupation. He was called in the panel "Mill Boss."

The 88th section of the Act of 14th April, 1834, relating to juries, requires the name, surname, addition, or occupation of jurors to be given, but this only for the purpose of identification. The provision is directory merely. And to be a mark of identity, it is necessary that the addition or occupation shall be written as it is commonly known in the community from which the juror is drawn. There is no question about the identity of this juror. It is not pretended that there is any other Mathew S. Ridgway in Montour county. His Christian and surnames, therefore, sufficiently indicate him; but lest some other man of the same name should be found, the statute required his addition or occupation to be expressed in the language in which it is commonly known. A precisely descriptive addition might not indicate him at all, simply because his neighbours were not accustomed so to think and speak of him. "Mill Boss," we take it for granted, was the popular designation of his occupation; and therefore it is quite immaterial whether the words are capable of strict definition as applicable to a rolling-mill, or a mill of any other description, they were the appropriate words for the occasion.

The fourth and last error assigned is for overruling the plea to the jurisdiction.

Counsel for the Commonwealth insists on calling it a mere challenge of the president judge, which they argue is not allowable. In form it is a special plea; and that the prisoner may have the full benefit of it, we will treat it as a plea to the jurisdiction. It denies that Judge Jordan, whom it recognises as "acting as president judge of the court here," was ever elected a judge of the Court of Oyer and Terminer of Montour county, agreeably to the constitution and laws of the Commonwealth; and alleges that Montour county, at the time of the election of judges, formed no part of Judge Jordan's district, but belonged to and formed part of the 11th judicial district, composed of the counties of Luzerne, Wyoming, Columbia, and Montour; and that Judge Conyngham was duly elected president judge of said district.

To this plea there was a demurrer, a joinder therein, and judgment for the Commonwealth. A very important question upon the constitutional power of the legislature so to alter judicial districts as to transfer a judge to the courts of certain counties who was never voted for in those counties, was intended to be raised by this plea; but, unfortunately for the prisoner, it cannot be raised in this form.

His plea admits that Judge Jordan is a judge de facto; and if it did not admit this, we would take judicial notice of the legislation which placed him in the courts of Montour county, so far as to hold him to be a judge de facto. That legislation is at least a colourable title to his office. Can the rights and powers of a judge de facto, with colour of title, be questioned in any other form than by quo warranto, at the suit of the Commonwealth? Assuredly not.

That a private relator could not test the validity of a judicial commission, even by quo warranto, was decided in Burrell's Case, 7 Barr 34, and the principle has been applied in a variety of other cases: see 7 S. # JR. 386; 2 Rawle 139; 16 S. $ R. 144; 2 W. $ S. 37; 8 Harris 415; 5 Mass. Rep. 230; 4 #?:« ^ Johnson 1; 10 5. £ 0. 230; 11 .Ad. ^ .E. 949.

But if a private suitor may not, by the appropriate process, question a judge's commission, when he has a chance to be heard in defence of his right, much less may such a suitor do it collaterally in an action to which the judge is not a party, and where he cannot be heard by himself or counsel.

If this defendant may plead to the jurisdiction of the judge, every defendant in Montour county, whether in civil or criminal proceedings, may do the same; and Judge Jordan, instead of trying the rights of parties, will be continually engaged in defending his own. Not merely in defending them, but in adjudicating them, contrary to that law, which is too elementary even for the bill of rights, that forbids a man to judge his own cause.

He is a judge de facto, and as against all parties but the Commonwealth, he is a judge de jure also. If the legislation complained of is to be tested, it must be at the instance of the Attorney-General or of some public officer representing the sovereignty of the state. The notion that the functions of a public officer, or of a corporation existing by authority of law, can be drawn in question (I do not mean as to the mode of their exercise, but as to their right of existence), except at the pleasure of the sovereign, is a mistake that springs from the too prevalent misconception that it is the duty of everybody to attend to public affairs. Public officers are provided for public duties, and the remedy for delinquencies is of frequent recurrence, is specific and effectual. This plea to the jurisdiction cannot avail the defendant, even to raise the constitutional question intended.

Having thus given deliberate attention to all the errors assigned upon the record, and to whatever was urged in their support, the painful duty only remains for us to pronounce the judgment affirmed.

PHOTO AND DOCUMENT CREDITS

Sketch of the Big Mill: Mordan, Larry E., Used with permission from the Mordan family

Puddlers: Photo from Helen (Sis) Hause

Montour County Jail: Photo from William W. Wilt III

Chalfant and Hughes Ad: Danville Intelligencer (1858)

Mary Twiggs Death Warrant: Pennsylvania State Archives

Wm. J. Clark Death Warrant: Pennsylvania State Archives

Grove Brothers Petition (Images 1-7): Pennsylvania State Archives

Handwritten notes of Rev J.W. Yeomans of Conversations with Mary Twiggs (Pages 2-3): Pennsylvania State Archives

Judge Alex Jordan Letter: Pennsylvania State Archives
Reverend J.W. Yeomans Letter: Pennsylvania State Archives

William F. Packer: Photo from Wikipedia

Wm. J. Clark vs the Commonwealth: The Unified Judicial System of Pennsylvania

WORKS CITED

CHAPTER ONE
Danville Intelligencer, 3 Sept. 1858, page 1.

"Execution of Mary Twiggs for the Murder of Catherine Ann Clark." *Sunbury American*, 30 Oct. 1858, page 3.

CHAPTER TWO
Mokyr, Joel. "Famine Ireland (1845- 1849)." *Encyclopaedia Britanica*, Accessed April 2020.

"Clark Passenger List Arrival on the Clydesdale."11 May 1851 *Ancestry.com*.

"David Twiggs and Mary McClintock Marriage: Family Search Website Record No: MZZQ-3CF." *Family Search*, Event Place: Convoy, Donegal, Ireland, 27 Jan. 1846.

"The Poisoning Cases." *Sunbury American (Pennsylvania Newspaper Archive-First Edition)*, 13 June 1857, page 2.

CHAPTER THREE
Brower, D. H. B. *Danville, Montour County, Pennsylvania: a Collection of Historical and Biographical Sketches,* 1881, page 186.

Davis, Rebecca Harding, "Life in the Iron-Mills," *The Atlantic Magazine*, 1861.

"The Murder Trial At Danville." *Sunbury American*, 27 Feb. 1858, page 2.

"The Poisoning Cases." *Sunbury American,* 13 June 1857, page 3.

CHAPTER FOUR
"Attempted Escape." *Danville Intelligencer, 11* Sept.1857, page 2.

"Attempted Escape." *The Sunbury Gazette,* 1 July 1858, page 2.

CHAPTER FIVE

Danville Intelligencer, 25 Dec. 1857, page 1.

"Duties of a Grand Jury." Wikipedia. Accessed February 2020

"Court." *Star of the North*, 30 Dec. 1857, page 2.

Danville Intelligencer, 25 Sept. 1857, page 1.

"The Montour Iron Company." *Danville Intelligencer*, 16 Oct. 1857, page 1.

CHAPTER SIX
Danville Intelligencer, 19 Feb. 1858, page 1.

"The Murder Trial at Danville." *Sunbury American*, 27 Feb. 1858, page 2.

"Murder Trial." *Columbia Democrat and Bloomsburg General Advertiser*, 27 Feb. 1858, page 2.

CHAPTER SEVEN
"The Murder Trial at Danville." *Sunbury American*, 27 Feb. 1858, page 2.

"Murder Trial." *Columbia Democrat and Bloomsburg General Advertiser*, 27 Feb. 1858, page 2.

CHAPTER EIGHT
"Comprising Cases Adjudged in the Supreme Court of Pennsylvania.*" PENNSYLVANIA STATE REPORTS VOL. XXIX.* Accessed May 2019.

Casey, Joseph. "1857 William John Clark versus the Commonwealth," Cases Decided in May and October Terms, 1857.

Danville Intelligencer, 21 May 1858, page 1.

"Trial of Mrs. Twiggs." *Sunbury American*, 29 May 1858, page 2.

CHAPTER NINE
Danville Intelligencer, 16 July 1858, page 1.

"Declaration of Wm. J. Clark.*" Sunbury Gazette*, 31 July 1858, page 3.

CHAPTER TEN
Danville Intelligencer, 6 Aug. 1858.

Danville Intelligencer, 3 Sept. 1858, page 1.

"The Execution of WM. J. Clark." *Danville Intelligencer*, 24 Sept. 1858, page 1.

"The Execution of Wm J. Clark." *Sunbury American*, 2 Oct. 1858, page 1.

CHAPTER ELEVEN
Danville Intelligencer, 1 Oct. 1858, page 1.

Yeomans, J. W., "Conversations Between Mary Twiggs and Reverend Doctor J.W. Yeomans," Pennsylvania State Archives.

CHAPTER TWELVE
Baldy, E. H., "Letter from E.H. Baldy Esq. to Governor Wm. F. Packer," Pennsylvania State Archives, June 1, 1858.

Grove, J. P. and John, "Letter from Judge Alexander Jordan to Governor Wm. F. Packer" 9 Oct. 1858, Pennsylvania State Archives.

Yeomans, J. W., "Letter from Rev. Dr. John W. Yeomans to Governor Wm. F. Packer" 7 Oct. 1858, Pennsylvania State Archives.

CHAPTER THIRTEEN
"Execution of Mary Twiggs." *Danville Intelligencer*, 29 Oct. 1858, page 1.

"Execution of Mary Twiggs For The Death of Catherine Ann Clark." *Sunbury American,* 30 Oct. 1858, page 3.

"Editorial on Twiggs Death." *Philadelphia Inquirer*, 23 Sept. 1858.

"Editorial." *Wisconsin Free Democrat*, 3 Nov. 1858.

"Editorial." *True American*, 10 Nov. 1858.

"Editorial." *Carlisle Weekly Herald*, 21 Nov. 1858.

ACKNOWLEDGEMENTS

I need to say thank you to a number of people and organizations that have provided information, insight and encouragement in the course of writing this book.

My friendship with Jean Knouse dates back a number of years when we took part in historical cemetery tours in the community. Jean painstakingly wrote the scripts for most of the participants, using her teaching skills to help all of us who took on the personas of people from Montour County's past. Jean was a logical choice as editor and graciously agreed to help me in writing, editing, and encouraging me along the way in this project. Taking a radio news reporter who has spent a career condensing stories into headlines, and helping him stretch them into a book, has been no easy task for Jean.

The staff at the Pennsylvania State Archives in Harrisburg provided their expertise in finding records such as the death warrants of William John Clark and Mary Twiggs. Letters containing pleas for a pardon and an eye-opening interview between accused killer Mary Twiggs and spiritual adviser Reverend J.W. Yeomans preserved for more than 160 years were valuable pieces of the story.

Special thanks must also be extended to my history loving friends, especially Helen (Sis) Hause and Lynn Reichen, who have added their encouragement during the writing of the book. And finally, to my wife Ann, who kept prodding, pestering, and asking if I had worked on "the book" lately. During several times when I became discouraged and thought about abandoning the project, she helped me see the path forward.

Finally, a special thanks must be extended to Greg Laird and Cooper Street Imaging LLC. Greg's expertise turned documents that are more than 160 years old, such as the Twiggs and Clark death warrants, into legible materials found inside this book. Greg painstakingly clarified various petitions including the Grove Brothers, notes of conversations between Mary Twiggs and her and spiritual adviser Reverend J.W. Yeomans. Among the letters Greg made legible was one from presiding Judge Alex Jordan to

Pennsylvania Governor William Packer Fisher, in which Judge Jordan questions the Twiggs conviction based on testimony presented at her trial.

Greg worked closely with me in designing the cover for the book. In addition to his digital imaging company, he is also a federal licensed drone pilot.

Friends and colleagues are special people in our lives, but they are "treasures" when you are writing a book.

Cooper Street Imaging, LLC

Gregory Laird, Owner

946 Cooper Street
Danville, PA 17821
(570) 594-8342
cooperstreetimaging.com
cooperstreetimaging@gmail.com

ABOUT THE AUTHOR

Terry Diener was born in Lebanon, Pennsylvania. A graduate of Northern Lebanon High School, he went on to both broadcasting school in Washington D.C. and radio engineering school in Fredericksburg, Virginia. In 2018, Terry was proud to be chosen an honorary Alum of Danville High School.

Terry began his radio career in 1971 and has worked in newsrooms throughout eastern Pennsylvania as a radio reporter and news director. Early in his career he was a news stringer for the Patriot News in Harrisburg and a small weekly in northeastern Pennsylvania. He currently serves as the Pennsylvania news correspondent for Family Life Network headquartered in Bath, New York.

His love for local history has led to numerous newspaper articles and in-depth research at Pennsylvania's State Archives in Harrisburg and the National Archives in Washington D.C.

Terry regularly portrays and shares the life story of Colonel Charles Eckman of the 93rd Pennsylvania Infantry Regiment. Several years ago, Terry compiled a small book entitled "To See What I Have Seen: Montour County Men in the Civil War."

He has been involved in Danville's Iron Heritage Festival for a number of years, taking part in the popular cemetery tours. and at the Montour County Historical Society's Montgomery House Museum. He is a former board member and secretary for the Historical Society and is a regular contributor to the Montour County Historical and Genealogical Society newsletters.

Terry resides in Montour County with his wife Ann.